12/18

PROPOSITION 13 – AMERICA'S SECOND GREAT TAX REVOLT

PROPOSITION 13 – AMERICA'S SECOND GREAT TAX REVOLT: A FORTY YEAR STRUGGLE FOR LIBRARY SURVIVAL

BY

CHARLES I. GUARRIA

Long Island University, Brooklyn, USA

United Kingdom – North America – Japan – India – Malaysia – China

Emerald Publishing Limited
Howard House, Wagon Lane, Bingley BD16 1WA, UK

First edition 2019

Reprints and permissions service
Contact: permissions@emeraldinsight.com

British Library Cataloguing in Publication Data
A catalogue record for this book is available from the British Library

ISBN: 978-1-78769-018-9 (Print)
ISBN: 978-1-78769-017-2 (Online)
ISBN: 978-1-78769-019-6 (Epub)

ISOQAR certified
Management System,
awarded to Emerald
for adherence to
Environmental
standard
ISO 14001:2004.

Certificate Number 1985
ISO 14001

INVESTOR IN PEOPLE

Dedication

To Donna Regan who lovingly sat by my side through many hours in both libraries and bookstores, and who patiently read innumerable snippets. Love you!!!

Contents

Chapter 1

1978–1979: In the Beginning

The maximum amount of any ad valorem tax on real property shall not exceed one percent (1%) of the full cash value of such property. The one percent (1%) tax to be collected by the counties and apportioned according to law to the districts within the counties. (Howard Jarvis Taxpayers Association, 2018)

These words became law in California on July 1, 1978, the start of the fiscal year, by virtue of a June 6, 1978 vote that saw 4,280,689 people (64.8%) voting in favor and 2,326,167 people (35.2%) voting against with a ratio of 1.8:1 ("California Proposition 13, Tax Limitations Initiative 1978," n.d.). The measure passed in all but three counties. The voting public in California gave life to the People's Initiative to Limit Property Taxation, otherwise known as Proposition 13, the shot heard 'round the land. A tax and expenditure limitation wrapped in a proposition, proposed as an amendment to the California state constitution to be known lawfully as Article XIIIA (Tax Limitation; Sections 1–7).

For the sake of context, in 1978, property taxes were a significant source of revenue for California's local governments. They accounted for 36.3% of county revenues, 22.4% of city revenues, and 67.4% of non-enterprise special district revenues (Simon, 1998). Special districts are independent forms of local government created by the community to meet a specific need. Be it new services or higher levels of existing services. The community forms the special district to pay for and administer the service. Many libraries were located within high-property tax-dependent special districts.

Proposition 13 was backed by a movement that set out to cut California's property tax rate. It was successful; after passage, a typical homeowner's property tax bill fell from $900 to $400, a 55.6% decrease (Willis, 1981). Statewide, property taxes were cut an average of 57% (Willis, 1981). The proposition limited real property taxes to 1% of full cash value except as necessary to pay for previously incurred voter-approved debt. Property taxes were to be collected by counties and apportioned according to state government law. This granting to the state government the power of the purse strings led to a diminution in the ability of local government to control its own affairs. The new law required property to be valued

Proposition 13 – America's Second Great Tax Revolt:
A Forty Year Struggle for Library Survival, 1–37
Copyright © 2019 by Emerald Publishing Limited
doi:10.1108/978-1-78769-017-220181001

as of March 1, 1975 or at the date of change of ownership (to include vacation homes) or construction if such date is on or after March 1, 1975. Subsequent increases were tied to the consumer price index not to exceed 2% per annum. State and local governments were prohibited from imposing any additional property, sales, or transaction taxes on the sale of real property; it required a two-thirds vote in each house of the legislature to increase or impose new state taxes and a two-thirds vote of the "qualified electors" to increase or add new local special-purpose taxes. The two-thirds super majority requirement allowed for a small minority of one-third plus one the ability to block the vote. The proposition was amended in November 1978 by Proposition 8 to allow for property reassessments due to a declining housing market or a decline in value due to disaster.

> Vote yes on Proposition 13 and send a message to tens of thou-
> sands of teachers, librarians, firefighters, police officers, sanitation
> workers and public-health specialists that you can safely dispense
> with their services. (Los Angeles Times, *Editorial, May 1978*)

Challenged from the beginning and questioned throughout its history. Shortly after passage, Proposition 13's constitutionality was put into question. The Amador Valley Joint Union High School District brought suit against the State Board of Education claiming that Proposition 13 was a revision of the state constitution and not an amendment. The state supreme court confirmed that an initiative couldn't revise the constitution; however, Proposition 13 was an amendment to the California constitution and not a revision (*Amador Valley Joint Union High School District* v. *State Board of Equalization*, 2017). Within this ruling was a set of protocols utilized by other courts when they considered ambiguous language within Proposition 13 (Cole, 1998). Mr. Howard Jarvis, one of two key players in the initiation of Proposition 13, noted that if Proposition 13 had been ruled unconstitutional, he would have had to "call for a statewide revolt against paying property taxes" (Jarvis & Pack, 1979).

It was argued that cutting the property tax would merely result in raising the income tax. That such a move simply shifts the tax burden from one type of tax to another. Although a property tax cut would be beneficial for retirees, raising the income tax would be harmful to those who typically received income tax relief: low wage earners and renters. Businesses would also gain from a property tax cut, although they too could see a mere shift of taxes to a higher corporate tax. Proponents of Proposition 13 argued that its passage was necessary to keep businesses within California and to make the state more attractive to new businesses.

Many believed that Proposition 13 would aid people who need relief from economic hardship the least and restrict access to learning materials for people ill equipped to afford the cost of purchasing said materials. By way of example, if a city were to close a library, those in the higher income brackets likely would have books and educational material to read or have access to them. Additionally, these same households will receive a large tax break. Those in the lower tax brackets, in most cases, did not have access to reading or educational material and will not receive as big a tax break.

That angry noise was the sound of a middle-class tax revolt erupting and its tremors are shaking public officials from Sacramento to Washington D.C. (Time, 1978c)

Termed as the most emotional issue to sweep across the state in a generation, *Time* magazine described Proposition 13 as hitting like a cross between a tidal wave and an earthquake. It was the first major tax cap in American history and an interesting development put in context of the present view of California as the tax me more state.

It took California from a high tax state to an average tax state. It was considered a bell weather of the widespread tax revolt in America in the late 1970s[1,2] helping to shape President Ronald Reagan's message that government was the problem not the solution.[3] Proposition 13 was often mentioned as one of two most widely publicized first world tax revolts of the twentieth century. The other being the founding of Denmark's Progress Party in 1972[4] (Danziger, 1980). Some argued that Proposition 13 was a continuation of a tax revolt, rather than a beginning. They pointed to Alabama governor George C. Wallace in 1972, California governor Ronald Reagan in 1973, and presidential nominee Jimmy Carter in 1976 as examples of politicians who had seized on anti-tax rhetoric prior to Proposition 13.

The surface issue was, of course, the property tax cut. There was an underlying issue that voters faced: a vote for Proposition 13 was a vote for limiting the funds available to the government, thus limiting the activities and size of the government. On its 30th anniversary, Mr. Ted Costa, the head of People's Advocate,[5] underscored the point: "The overwhelming opinion was that the purpose of Prop. 13 was to limit the size of government" (Wildermuth, 2008).

Californians voted for the proposition despite the predicted financial restrictions it would place on state and local governments. The predictions indicated drastic cuts to public services (termed a fiscal *hara-kiri*) and mass layoffs, to include libraries, would follow such a vote. The degree to which a library system would be affected varied based on the dependency to property taxes for funding. Some systems had very little dependency on property taxes, while others had near complete dependency on property taxes.

Mr. Howard Jarvis, one of the two men responsible for Proposition 13, considered these dire warnings "a snow job by marinated bureaucrats and over-animated popcorn balls" (Knapp, 1998). Speaking specifically about libraries he

---

[1]This movement received a push by the American Tax Reduction Movement, a unit within the Howard Jarvis Taxpayers Association.

[2]Columnist George F. Will agreed, stating that Proposition 13 was the impetus for "the conservative decade" 1978–1988.

[3]President Ronald Reagan, who served two terms, 1967–1971 and 1971–1975, as California governor before Proposition 13, was an enthusiastic supporter of the proposition.

[4]Historically, anti-tax sentiment can be traced back to 70 AD when the Jewish population refused to pay a temple tax to the Romans.

[5]Founded by Mr. Paul Gann, one of two key players in the initiation of Proposition 13.

stated: "I happen to feel it is not a hardship to have libraries closed two out of every seven days; people still have plenty of opportunities to use them" (White, 2011). He also felt that kids did not read anymore – making libraries less valuable.

It was the public's feeling that local governments would absorb the reduced revenue, with little change occurring to essential services. However, when presented with 15 spending areas that could be cut, 58% of voters responded that they would prefer spending cuts in no more than three of the 15 areas. Half of these voters supported Proposition 13. This illustration of not wanting cuts when given specifics yet still favoring Proposition 13 indicated a level of frustration voters held with regard to their rising property tax bill. The public's frustration did not spillover to libraries, as a CBS News/*Los Angeles Times*-administered poll showed that a mere 4% of respondents favored cuts in libraries.

> It is, in many respects, a legitimate grassroots populist revolt against the stupidity of government. But it clearly favors the large land owners and property owners … (It is) the death of the New Deal.
> – Tom Hayden on Proposition 13 (Broder, 1978)

No matter the age, income, geographic location, or party affiliation, the initiative won the majority. As a rule, homeowners are more likely to favor property tax limitations than renters are. However, renters, along with those who had public employees in to their family, and African Americans, did vote for the proposition in higher numbers than expected: 47%, 44%, and 42% respectively (Danziger, 1980), giving the appearance of a coming together of self-interest (a tax reduction) and principle (limiting government).

Simply put, many Californians believed that it was time to contain the extensive growth of both public expenditures and the tax system. Adding to the people's frustration was the fragmented nature of local governments. The Advisory Commission on Intergovernmental Relations referred to this as the metropolitan problem – a complex and often confusing overlap of governments and functional responsibilities, producing serious obstacles to the clear political accountability of public officials or even of specific public agencies. Some of the governmental fragmentations were expected to abate after Proposition 13 was passed. It was believed that county governments would absorb special districts and provide services to the people within those special districts. Other special districts were not to be absorbed by county government, yet would be closely controlled. Additionally, inter-local arrangements were created between special districts to realize economies of scale when contracting for services.

A motivating cause for the tax revolt that spread through the United States of America in the years following Proposition 13 was a hope to create a more efficient government. Californian's frustration with their government was exemplified by the fact that the state could not discern how much of a budget surplus it had. The best they could do was to estimate a range of $3–6 billion[6] (Danziger, 1980).

---

[6]The surplus was the result of growth in California's computer, aerospace, and agricultural industries.

This led many Californians to believe their government was less than efficient in the area of fiscal management. Further, having that much of a budget surplus gave the impression that the state could not spend all the tax money it was collecting making a tax cut all the more plausible. To be clear, not every Californian felt that Proposition 13 would lead to a more efficient government. Some held the belief that centralizing would occur, resulting in a weakening of both competitive efficiency and diversity in the purchasing of public goods.

From the time of America's colonial period (1492–1763), property taxes have been a source for raising revenue. During that period, city hall, county courthouses, and school boards were typical of the type of institutions to receive funding. Today the list has been expanded to include libraries, firefighters, infrastructure, parks, police, public transportation, and recreation.[7]

Since 1911, Californians could affect their own taxes through the use of referendum. Attempts to use referendums in this manner are often referred to as populism. Appealing to the citizenry with a populist message proved effective for the southern California businessmen behind Proposition 13: Mr. Howard Arnold Jarvis and Mr. Paul Gann.[8] How exactly did these two gentlemen motivate the California voter? Mr. Jarvis stated: "We learned the best approach to use on someone when you want to get their signature on a petition (was) 'Sign this it will help lower your taxes,' that usually worked." The use of effective mailings was also part of their strategy. Mr. Jarvis commented that the most effective mailing "told every property owner how much his tax bill was, how much he would save on 13 in one year, and how much he'd save in five years" (Martin, 2006). Further helping to convince the citizenry of the proposition's benefits was its easily understood design.

Of course speaking directly to the voter was a key element and came easy for the ever-verbose Mr. Jarvis. He was not immune to stump speeches in which he would explain that this was the peoples chance to tell the government no more "Tax, tax, tax; spend, spend, spend; re-elect, re-elect, re-elect" (Coupal, 2016). He would put emphasis on fair taxes, equal for everybody, and "within the ability of the people who were taxed to pay for it" (Jarvis & Pack, 1979).

In the early 1960s, Californians were known to self-identify as living in a cheerful place with professional workers, raising young families with access to a growing, robust library system. By 1978, the typical voter and supporter of Proposition 13 was a mix of affluent middle-aged homeowners, possibly retired, having older children who were not availing themselves of public services such as libraries, parks, playgrounds, and schools.

Importantly, with regard to Proposition 13, the 1978 Californian was struggling with the rising cost of property taxes that were slightly above the national average.

---

[7]Neither list for the colonial period nor for the present day is meant to be all-inclusive. They are illustrative of how property taxes have been allocated and expanded throughout American history.

[8]Economist Arthur Laffer fully supported the initiative and has been given credit for helping to write it despite a lack of evidence to support a writing credit (Wikipedia, 2018).

Naturally Mr. Howard Jarvis and Mr. Paul Gann profiled more with the typical voter and supporter of Proposition 13 than the typical early 1960s Californian.

Mr. Jarvis (1903–1986) was 74 years old on June 6, 1978, the day Proposition 13 was approved. Among the jobs held by the millionaire ex-businessman (*The Globe and Mail*, 1986) was executive director of both the Apartment Association of Los Angeles County and the United Organization of Taxpayers. ("California Voters Pass Initiative Cutting Taxes by 57%," *Facts on File World News Digest*, 1978).

In 1980, Mr. Jarvis professed no allegiance to either the Republican Party or the Democratic Party, although he was a "rock-ribbed Republican" until 1962 (Scherer, 1980). Born in Utah ("Howard Jarvis Millionaire led revolt against property tax," *The Globe and Mail*, 1986), he became a resident of West Los Angeles California ("Sound and fury over taxes Howard Jarvis and the voters send a message," *Time*, 1978) and a runner-up for *Time*'s Man [*sic.*] of the Year (Coupal, 2010). He also had numerous unsuccessful runs for public office; a 1962 Republican nomination for United States Senate and several attempts at the mayorship of Los Angeles ("Howard Jarvis," Wikipedia, 2018b).

Mr. Paul Gann (1912–1989) was born in Arkansas and settled in the Sacramento, California area (McQuiston, 1989). He was a few days short of his 66th birthday on June 6, 1978, the date Proposition 13 was approved. Among the jobs held by Mr. Gann were real estate salesman and auto salesman (McQuiston, 1989). Along the way he became a political activist forming and then heading an anti-tax lobby group called People's Advocate (*Facts on File World News Digest*, 1978). In 1980, Mr. Gann lost a bid for the United States Senate to Mr. Alan Cranston ("Paul Gann," Wikipedia, 2018d).

Reaction and Rally Cry for and Against Proposition 13

> I wanted to stop 13. I ended up in the hospital after debating Jarvis all over the state. – Los Angeles County Supervisor Mr. Edmund D. Edelman recalling the effort against Proposition 13. (Scott, 2003)

It did indeed seem to be the most emotional issue to sweep across the state in more than a generation. Associations, businesses, governmental agencies, individuals, and organizations all began to release information detailing either the ills or the virtues of the proposition.

The Bank of America, the California Chamber of Commerce, Democrats, the League of Women Voters, newspapers,[9] renters, Republicans, school administrators, and unions (including the American Federation of Teachers), all rallied to oppose the proposition. The Los Angeles Chamber of Commerce believed

---

[9]The *Valley News and Green Sheet* was a leading anti-Proposition 13 newspaper. In 1981, the paper changed its name to the *Daily News of Los Angeles*.

Proposition 13 to be "a fraud on the taxpayer that will cause fiscal chaos, massive unemployment and disruption of the economy" (Carpay, 2003). Governor Jerry Brown joined those opposing calling it "a rip-off" (Hazlett, 1978), warning the current tax situation was "the evil you know" and that was better than "the evil you don't know" (White, 2011). Further, he believed that he would vote for Proposition 13 "if I were a communist" (Carpay, 2003).

San Diego mayor Mr. Peter Wilson, who later served two terms as governor of California from 1991 to 1999 and Los Angeles mayor, Mr. Thomas Bradley were adamantly opposed. Mr. Bradley stated, the proposition would "hit the city like a neutron bomb, leaving some city facilities standing virtually empty and human services devastated" (Carpay, 2003).

San Francisco mayor Mr. George Moscone cautioned: "Our police, our libraries, our fire department, and schools would be crippled" ("Between the Pigs and the Swill," *Time*, 1978a). He went on to say that he would "lock the library doors" if Proposition 13 were to pass ("The Time to Start Was Yesterday," *Journal of Academic Librarianship*, 1978).

That warning "scared me," stated Ms. Karen Scannell, a San Francisco branch head librarian. It scared her enough that she had initiated plans to close the library (Plotnick, 1978). Simultaneously, library supporters in San Francisco made plans to try and keep the library open. In conjunction with city librarian Mr. John Frantz, they created bookmarks, posters, and signs that were made available throughout the library, detailing the ramifications that the passage of Proposition 13 would bring to include the closing of branch libraries.

Kevin Star, a former San Francisco librarian who had transitioned to columnist for the San Francisco Examiner, responded to the utilization of posters, stating it was "ideological concubinage … like any old whore the library will be cast aside now that the mayor's one-night stand is over" (Berry, 1978b). Not only was the San Francisco Public Library (SFPL) not cast aside, it was relied on more, as Proposition 13 forced the closing of a recreational facility within the Sunset District requiring users of the facility to patronize the nearby Ortega Branch Library.

The SFPL awareness campaign also asked, in light of possible branch closings, to return books on or before Friday, June 30, 1978. There was a sign in front of the main library informing that the main library would be closing on June 30 if Proposition 13 were to pass. Although that was an idle threat, the main library did stay open after the proposition was passed, the tactics on the whole were effective as the proposition did not receive the majority of votes in San Francisco.

A local judge stopped a plan of Los Angeles County workers to put notices on 5,000 public buildings, including libraries and museums. These notices were to inform the people that the building might be closed if Proposition 13 was passed.

The Los Angeles Public Library (LAPL) created a budget based on the proposition's expected cuts, known as the Jarvis Budget. It showed the closure of 16 branches accompanied by the firing of 800 employees. Without regard for a library system that had been open since 1873, Mr. Jarvis, when asked about libraries closing in Los Angeles because of Proposition 13, commented: "It doesn't bother me a damn bit … most of the children they are for can't read. And I don't know what the hell good it does to have the books there. Now I understand they're closing one day a week. Which doesn't bother me at all. I have been familiar with libraries for some time. Ninety percent of the time you could shoot a cannon through and nobody's there" (Berry, 1978b).

Speaking of libraries in general Mr. Jarvis stated: "And if a library here and there has to close Wednesday mornings between 9 and 11, life will go on. Who the hell goes to the library in the morning, anyway?" (Citrin, 2009). Supporters of the proposition stated those who use libraries could afford to pay for the privilege.

One month before the proposition was to be voted on the *Los Angeles Times* (*LA Times*) reported that Los Angeles County would have to close half of the 93 branches if the proposition was voted up. (Note, there are two library systems in Los Angeles: the County of Los Angeles Public Library [CoLAPL] and the city's Los Angeles Public Library [LAPL]).

The city of Los Angeles took the extreme measure of publishing a list of 37,000 people who could potentially be dismissed, based on seniority, if the proposition passed. Similarly, The Los Angeles Board of Education and other school boards sent termination notices to thousands of teachers who might conceivably be fired. Not in a direct response to the Los Angeles Board of Education, rather as a matter of statement regarding Proposition 13's possible damaging effects on schools, Mr. Jarvis had commented: "The initiative is to cut property taxes in California and to save a couple of million people from losing their homes. They are a lot more important than twenty thousand schoolteachers" (Martin, 2006).

Librarians had been apprised that 60% of the state's libraries might have to close ("Revolt over taxes aroused California voters confront a beguiling proposition," *Time*, 1978b). These closures would contribute to the higher unemployment estimated by the University of California, Los Angeles (UCLA) Business Forecasting Project. They believed that Proposition 13 would push the unemployment rate from 7.3% to 10.1% (*Time*, 1978b). If this were to happen, the net result would be an increased use of public services at a time that those very services were receiving less funding. Not an uncommon occurrence within libraries where economic hardship, in this case being out of work, typically heightens the public's awareness to the free and beneficial services provided by the public library.

The predicted deleterious effect that Proposition 13 was to have on unemployment proved erroneous. One year after passage, California's unemployment rate dropped from 7.3% to 6.3%. It did reach 10% four years after passage, 1982, and then proceeded a steady decline to a low of 5.2% in 1989 not to reach the predicted 10.1% mark until the near end of the great recession, specifically 2009, when unemployment climbed to 11.3% ("California Unemployment Statistics", Wikipedia, 2006).

The reality of how funding was affecting libraries was not only a big city concern. Carpinteria is a small city located 15 minutes south of Santa Barbara along US 101 on the California coast. Head librarian Mr. Mark King said, "If Jarvis passes I know we will lose our two part-time assistants. And if we aren't closed down entirely they will certainly cut down on the library hours" (Kool, 1978). Mr. King went on to say that both he and his associate were willing to reduce their salaries if it meant keeping the library open (Kool, 1978).

In an attempt to stop Mr. Jarvis and Mr. Gann and possibly winning votes for the coming election, Governor Jerry Brown sponsored a rival proposition that he termed, "the greatest tax-cut package ever produced in the United States" (*Time*, 1978b). Proposition 8 was backed by the "No on Proposition 13 Committee." The committee was made up of the state legislature, the American Federation of Labor and Congress of Industrial Organizations (A.F.L.–C.I.O), Southern California Edison, the Federated Fire Fighters, and the Sierra Club. It would allow residential properties to be taxed at a lower rate than other property types. It would produce an average property tax cut of 30% as opposed to the 57% under Proposition 13. There would be no tax cut to commercial landowners, give renters an annual $75 cash rebate, limit future property tax increases to the rate of inflation, and tie the future growth of local and state government spending to the growth in average personal income. Further, it would transfer money to local governments to make up for the funds they would lose because of this (Proposition 8's) proposed property-tax cut (*Time*, 1978b).

Proposition 8 could not gain voter attention; it was too little, too late, and too complicated, making it too hard to explain. Polls showed when a voter knew of both Proposition 13 and Proposition 8, they preferred Proposition 8. Put rather well by the *Los Angeles Times'* Mr. George Skelton (2012): "In the minds of most voters, Proposition 8 still is a mystery."

Lastly, the success of Proposition 8 was conditional. It needed Proposition 13 to lose for it to win. Had they both been adopted (gained a majority vote), Proposition 13 would have prevailed. This is due to the fact that it was a "popular referendum" and as such would be given precedence over Proposition 8, a proposed constitutional amendment.

The California State Library (CSL) (1978) proclaimed, there would be $7–8 billion[10] in lost local tax revenue in the first year of Proposition 13 and warned that, "the elimination of many services would be the inevitable result." This warning fell in line with the library community strategy to inform the public of the negative outcomes that would come from the propositions' passage as opposed to focusing public attention on the benefits afforded by libraries to the community at large.

The dysfunction within the California state government was another factor leading the people of California to knowingly vote for a bill that could adversely affect public services as warned by the CSL. Californians believed that an indifferent, self-serving bureaucracy had also become inefficient and incapable, or unwilling, to solve the state's problems.

The inefficiency was magnified by multiple tax relief bills that came before the California state legislature, of which not one was passed, including 22 property tax reform bills in 1977 and Proposition 8, the tax cut proposition backed by Governor Jerry Brown in 1978. Adding to the people's perception of their government's inefficiency was state's uncontrollable spending and growth. In the

---

[10]Typical property tax revenue collected was $11.4 billion per annum.

preceding 20 years, the state population had grown from 14 million to 22 million, an increase of 57.1%. Over the same time period, state employees grew at a rate of 500%, and the cost of running the municipal government grew at a rate of 689% (Brodie, 1978).

One needs to reach back to 1911 to find when the citizens of California were empowered with the ability to consider an initiative such as Proposition 13. With the strong backing of the Progressive Party and California Republican Governor Mr. Hiram Johnson (he served as governor from 1911 to 1917), initiative, referendum, and recall were added to the California Constitution in 1911. This was the byproduct of a movement that saw the federal government as insulated, unable to rally for a common purpose, and at the whim of special interests. Ironically, many believe that California's fiscal issues can be traced to initiatives and referendums that have "immobilized" the state with "incompatible demands" (Adler, 2010).

Conventional wisdom posits that voting behavior is strongly influenced by the individual's cost-benefit calculations. In this case, the short-term tax burden perception. If the perceived benefit of the tax (i.e., public service received) is proportional to the tax itself, the public accepts the tax as a benefit tax and will not become disillusioned to the payment of it. In reference to the point of being disillusioned, it is undeniable that Californians were experiencing skyrocketing inflation with regard to their housing costs. In fact, they were witness to some of the greatest increases in housing costs in the nation. Californians were paying property taxes that were approximately 52% above the national average. Inflation and a growing population left Californians with property values approximately three times the national average. These property values and the accompanying tax increases had risen 61% in the five years leading up to the vote on Proposition 13. After paying their income, property, and sales tax, the average household had spent more on the government than on their house, car, and food combined. Complicating the issue, personal income was not rising to meet the increased tax bills. The overall tax rate increased from approximately 11.3% of state personal income in the 1960s to 15.4% in 1978.

In the 15 years leading up to Proposition 13, tax rates increased by 51%, by the end of the 1970s some in California had been witness to a doubling of their property tax bill. Through the 1970s, people increasingly moved into the state. This created a housing shortage that initiated a rise in property values leading to reassessments that in some cases tripled. This resulted in higher property taxes that enabled government to enjoy a quadrupling of collected property taxes. Predictions held that if Proposition 13 had not passed, Californians would have experienced a near doubling of their tax bill over the four-year period of 1974–1978. Concern existed for first-time homebuyers, as the increasing tax levies made it difficult to assess the affordability of purchasing a house.

Several weeks before Proposition 13 passed, *Time* magazine reported that homeowners in California received assessments that in many cases were increase of 100% and in a few cases as much as 1,000% (*Time*, 1978b).

California's assessed property values were rising at an annual rate of 10–20% statewide, with some areas increasing 40% within a year. Among the hardest hit by these circumstances were the elderly and handicapped, many of whom were driven out of their homes, unable to pay their property taxes.

Housing inflation was one aspect that led to the passage of Proposition 13. Overall inflation rising at an annual rate of 10% was another. This drove taxpayers into higher marginal tax brackets on both state and federal levels.

By way of example, a resident who earned $22,000 in 1953 paid 1.1% in state income tax and 20.4% at the federal rate for a combined 21.5%. Inflation's effect by 1977 would have that same citizen earning $50,000 paying 5.6% in state income tax and 21.1% at the federal level for a combined 26.7%. In raw dollars, that is, $4,730 in 1953 and $13,350 in 1977.[11] The government of California was unable to react to this rise in inflation through tax relief, or by limiting spending; fueling the belief that government spending was out of control. A 1978 field poll found that 30% of respondents believed high taxes were "one of the most pressing issues in the state or community" (Throckmorton, 1997). These factors provided further motivation for the people to pass the proposition.

> *In spite of warnings, nothing much happens until the status quo becomes more painful than change.*
> *– Lawrence J. Peter (Reiss, 2014)*

The status quo had become untenable for the people of California. Citizens in other states latched on to this sentiment to create their own in-state tax rebellion. How effective, long-lasting, or far-reaching this tax rebellion would be was to be determined. An important consideration would be the perception of how disruptive Proposition 13 would be to governmental activities. That consideration required a wait and see approach. In the meantime, uncertainty remained in place. As former CBS newsperson Mr. Daniel Schorr stated, "This may, like the Boston Tea party, be the start of a general tax rebellion. Or it could just turn out to be a storm that will spend itself on the hard rocks of closed firehouses and closed libraries" (*Library Journal*, 1978b).

Those in favor of Proposition 13 were able to connect their thoughts on property taxes and government inefficiency with many across the country. In 1974, the Advisory Commission on Intergovernmental Relations found 45% of Americans indicated that property taxes were considered the least fair tax followed by federal income tax (19%) state income tax (13%), state sales tax (13%), and don't know (10%).

A 1978, Yankelovich poll revealed that 78% of Americans believed "Government wastes a lot of money we pay in taxes" (Baer, 2008). That was an eighteen-point jump from 1968. This backed the belief that the national tax revolt message was not only aimed at cutting taxes but also to reduce excessive government spending. The similarities between Californians and the rest of the country did not end with these desires. Inflation was yet another area that the national experience was similar to that of California. That being a quickly rising inflation rate. Inflation

---

[11]Example provided by the Advisory Commission on Intergovernmental Relations.

in the United States 10 years prior to Proposition 13 was 4.2%. It rose to a high of 13.5% in 1980 and steadily went down to 4.1% 10 years after the proposition passed, 1988 ("Historical Inflation Rates: 1914–2018," US Inflation Calculator, 2015). With each vote in favor of reform US citizens were making a statement that the burden of taxation outweighed the benefits of public services. Between 1970 and 1978, 19 states had imposed some measure of property tax limitation on their local government. In the November 1978 elections, 13 states voted on fiscal limitations, 10 were adopted. Four of the 13 were similar to Proposition 13; two of the four were passed. Seven of the states voted on what were considered less extreme measures. While other states and Congress considered fiscal limitations, including a balanced budget amendment to the US constitution (Danziger, 1980).

The main comment made by proponents of Proposition 13 after "taxes are too high" was "the time has come to cut government costs, waste, and inefficiency" (Danziger, 1980). Within the 1978 California Voter Pamphlet, proponents of the proposition used the statistic that 15% of all governmental spending is wasted. They included examples such as limousines for elected officials and huge pensions for governmental officials. The proposition's proponents suggested that Proposition 13 was a chance to "trade waste for property tax relief" and would prevent spendthrift politicians from taxing California into poverty.

In a poll one year prior to its passage California state residents viewed high taxes as the number one problem faced by the state and within their communities. While another poll, also one year out, had a 2:1 margin in favor of a smaller government providing fewer services. As Assemblyman Mr. Bill Leonard stated that the people were able "to not only complain about their taxes, but to do something about them. It redefined the relationship between taxpayers and government" (Cole, 1998).

Mr. Stephen Bauer, president of the Oregon League (Oregon faced a tax limitation bill in the Fall of 1978), believed that the scare tactics in California backfired. Warnings of drastic cutbacks only provided fuel to an angry citizenry, who knew California's budgetary surplus was in the billions. In fact, some held the belief that the billion dollar plus budget surplus itself served as a motivator to pass the proposition.

Economist Mr. Milton Freidman writing in *Newsweek* (1978) stated, "Despite the use of scare tactics, including notices to teachers of automatic dismissal on passage of Jarvis-Gann [Prop. 13], advance local budgets threatening drastic cuts in police and fire protection, and whatever other portents of catastrophe desperate feeders at the public trough could devise, the public refused to be bamboozled this time, as they had so often before while watching taxes mount and government services deteriorate. This time, the scare tactics simply produced a backlash."

Another factor considered was the changing demographics within California. Scholars indicated that there was a shift in citizenry beginning with the 1950s of a mostly young, upwardly mobile, and family-oriented population to 1978 when the population skewed older[12] and mostly white. They no longer had

---

[12]Older voters were more likely to vote for Proposition 13.

children attending schools, parks, or libraries but had a great concern regarding rising property taxes. Conversely, children attending schools, parks, and libraries were non-white, many with single parents, thus lacking the voting numbers needed to stall or reign in tax limitation initiatives such as Proposition 13 (Schrag, 1988).

A year before Proposition 13, in 1977, funding libraries was a priority as the state authorized a $5 million statewide library network and a universal state library card that would provide library users enhanced access and services ("Grim Prospects in California," *Library Journal*, 1978d). However, the conversation redirected with the passage of Proposition 13 to the question: What changes, if any, should libraries be preparing for? Would the cuts be as drastic as the warnings stated? Public libraries across the state feared the worst as word came that the state was prioritizing public schools, county and city government. Libraries began looking more closely at cooperatives as a means of stretching budget dollars.

Librarians, library staff, and administrators could not rest, as they needed to prove or reestablish their value. One salvation came via the public support. Only 17% of the people who supported Proposition 13 thought it was acceptable to cut library funding. That number bettered welfare (69%), parks, museums, and recreation (33%), public transportation (21%), and schools (18%). The public deemed only police (4%) and fire departments (1%) as more worthy of avoiding budget cuts than libraries (Plotnick, 1978).

Within six months of the passage of Proposition 13, the California Library Association (CLA) began planning for the passage of new legislation. They created principles that would provide the outline for this legislation.

These principles included the following:

- State funding of basic library services.
- Free access to library materials.
- A minimum of state control.
- Local administration of public library services.

It was hoped that through the principle of local administration control, funds could be raised to provide more than the basic services. Basic services were deemed as buying books, free reference assistance, and free interlibrary loan.

A *Los Angeles Times* poll, 60 days into the new law, indicated that the people were not satisfied with the work the politicians had done. Sixty-three percent felt the politicians were trying to change Proposition 13 to the politician's liking. (In fact, in the decades to come many attempts and suggestions were made to change the proposition.) Twenty-five percent felt the politicians were carrying out the will of the people and 12% were not sure.

As illustrated, the debate was well under way regarding the merits, or lack thereof, of Proposition 13. In summation, those in favor of Proposition 13 spoke to a need to curtail property taxes and correct an inefficient and wasteful government.

Those in opposition warned of fiscal instability, layoffs, a lessening or cessation of certain government services and higher unemployment. The voter heard the warnings, yet the message did not create a ground swell of opposition against Proposition 13. As Mr. Robert J. Samuelson wrote in a 1979 *The National Journal* article: In effect, the voter reclaimed power by reclaiming their taxes. It was as if the voter had said: "You are correct, it will be a mess to cut $7–8 billion from the state budget." However, this is a mess created by and of the people, our mess. Not a mess created by an inefficient, dysfunctional bureaucracy.

As State Assemblyman, Mr. Paul Priolo found out: "Whenever I tell an audience that Jarvis will bring local government to a halt, all I see is smiling faces" (Hazlett, 1978).

The Results Are In

> City hall is filled with gloom as civil servants wait their doom.
> For the voters have spoken on Jarvis-Gann and left many of us
> for the garbage cann. – Anonymous (Time, 1978)

"We feed foreigners and welfare bums with our tax money and my neighbors, 100% Americans, lost their land. Does that make any sense?" (White, 2011). This was stated by a schoolteacher giving her rationalization for voting in favor of Proposition 13.

California librarians sided more with the poem above, found on the door of San Francisco's city hall after the vote was tallied, than with the quote. As they were seen with t-shirts that read: *California Libraries Jarvis-Canned.* The *Library Journal* called the proposition a disaster with hope. Their hope was that the proposition would be a unifier for the library community that at the time was fractious.

As mentioned earlier, the numerous attempts in the preceding years to pass property tax relief had failed. This time it was not even close. Despite all the warnings of cuts and closures to schools, libraries, and other public services, the people of California had had enough with high property taxes, government inefficiency, and wastefulness. The self-defined "pain in the ass" businessman Mr. Jarvis along with the less verbose retired real estate salesman, Mr. Gann directed a victory at the polls.[13]

Given the highly charged atmosphere surrounding the proposition, it was no surprise that a near record turnout came to the polls. In total, 6,606,856 people voted on Proposition 13 ("California Proposition 13 Tax Limitations Initiative," Ballotpedia, 1978). Those voting for it called it a message sent to the California state government. Seventy percent of whom felt that they would not have any

---

[13]Mr. Jarvis gave credit to Mr. James Earle Christo, who in 1978 was the vice-chairman of the United Organization of Taxpayers and served as both Mayor and on the City Council of Bellflower California from 1982 to 1986. In fact, Mr. Christo had a personalized license plate that read "YES ON 13."

reduction in government services, while 22% felt the state government was providing too many unnecessary services (*Time*, 1978c).

Mr. Jarvis stated, "Tonight was a victory against money, the politicians, the government. We have seen the trauma of high taxes on older people. When elderly people get those tax bills on their meager homes that demand another $1,500 a year, they get a cloud over their heads. Many of them give up the spirit and quietly die. One woman had a heart attack in front of me back in 1962 right in the assessor's office. That means something to me even the Russians don't do that, run people out of their homes for no reason. It is a goddamned crime. It is grand felony theft."

He went on to compare the moment with the Boston Tea Party, proclaiming, "We have a new revolution. We are telling the government, 'Screw you!'" (*Time*, 1978c).

> *I began my governorship with a pledge of no new state taxes. I've carried out that promise. I began the effort at government frugality, and what I hear out of this vote is that people want more of it.*
> *– Governor Jerry Brown (Facts on File World News Digest, 1978)*

The day after the vote was known as the "Black Wednesday," yet there was little time for politicians to mourn as the proposition was passed within weeks of the new fiscal year. The state moved quickly to be in compliance with the propositions' tenants and on time with the fiscal year deadline of July 1. Governor Jerry Brown issued the following statement after the results were announced: "We have our marching orders from the people. This is the strongest expression of the democratic process in a decade. (The proposition will be implemented) in the most human, sensitive way I can – and without raising state taxes to bail out the newly stricken local units of government." But he admitted, "Things will never be the same" (*Time*, 1978c).

On Black Wednesday, June 7, the Governor had instituted a statewide hiring freeze (Cannon, 1978). A bit later, he asked for a statewide salary freeze ("Coping with the Tax Cut California Eases the Impact with a $5 Billion Dollar Relief Fund," *Time*, 1978d). It was reported that as many as 400,000 people could be laid off (Plotnick, 1978). On June 8, he addressed the state legislature: "I appeal to you to rise above the partisan temptations, to work together as a body and to fashion a bill that keeps faith with the fiscal realities and the mood philosophy of the people that we serve" (Cannon, 1978).

He added that "major human tragedies" were avoidable if the legislature acted quickly (Cannon, 1978). What the governor wanted was the legislature to distribute the $5 billion budget surplus to local governments (Cannon, 1978). The budget surplus distribution did begin (*Time*, 1978d).

Governor Brown asked landlords to pass on tax saving to their tenants. He initiated a Committee on Government Reform that was charged with estimating the impact of the proposition. The state library and the CLA supplied needed data to this committee in an effort to shed light on how libraries would be affected.

Contra Costa librarian Mr. Clarence Walter did note that the initial round of data might paint a darker picture of what lied ahead compared with the reality the library would face.

American Libraries Magazine called Proposition 13 "a concussive jolt felt 'round the library world'" (Plotnick, 1978) and tried to ease that jolt by offering to list the name of anyone laid off – referred to as Proposition 13 victims – in the event that a colleague might know a job for them (Plotnick, 1978). The editor-in-chief of the *Library Journal* Mr. John Berry (1979a) wrote that Proposition 13 was the detonation of a bomb that would "destroy much of what was great of the state's public library system." The LAPL union issued the following statement regarding Proposition 13 in their newsletter *Communicator*: "Librarians ... adamantly reject any pay cut" and are "not giving up any benefits" (Proposition 13 Reaction, 1978).

Mr. Walters was a bit more optimistic for the immediate implications: "The initial impact won't be as cataclysmic this year as original reports." But what of a year from now? "Unless actions are taken, both internally and externally, to improve library financing and cost effectiveness between now and next June, we will be faced with the same crises situation we have witnessed the past three weeks" (Berry, Fletcher, Havens, & Nyren, 1978).

The *Library Journal's* Mr. John Berry, writing on the nationwide ramifications of the passage of Proposition 13: "Every assumption in our "library faith" in our arsenal in defense of free public libraries is under attack. Every essential service, every staff member, every penny we spend will be tested and if the California experience is any indication, many of these basics will not survive the attack."

Speaking directly on the plight of libraries at the 97th Annual American Library Association (ALA) Conference in Chicago, June 24–30 1978, Mr. Berry urged ALA to send the message to taxpayers that "libraries are worth it, we're the solution not the problem" (Berry et al., 1978).

Mr. Berry advocated for a rethinking and possible repositioning of the role of public libraries in America. Topics under consideration were as follows: how libraries network; is it useful to ally with the educational community or should libraries fight the "bloody swing" of the tax revolt on their own; how to curb the inclination to charge fees; should public libraries and school libraries merge; and how to argue against the use of volunteers over paid staff. He urged librarians to join the *Library Journal* staff in seeking out an understanding of a new way of thinking about government, specifically the movement to apply free market metrics as an evaluative tool for government services. Mr. Berry concluded by stating that the staff of the *Library Journal* will reach out to other disciplines and search within the library industry for this better understanding and publish articles that can facilitate "a new philosophy, rational, and defense of public library service" (Berry et al., 1978).

American Library Association's incoming president Mr. Russell Shank was concerned about knee jerk reactions to charging fees as a means of supporting budget shortfalls. He called this idea "preemptive capitulation" and reminded librarians to restate the fundamental principles of free library services[14]: "I don't foresee a quick and sudden demise of the library or public agencies in America. But neither do I think that we can continue a slow paced, low keyed, stance in defense of what the library is to its constituents in and among the new media, new means of communication, and new agencies in the information age. I think it would be prudent to make a statement of affirmation of the America library philosophy soundly, forthrightly, and quickly. And I believe that the American Library Association has an obligation to mobilize the resources for this statement" (Berry et al., 1978).

In its coverage of the 97th Annual American Library Conference, the *Library Journal* (1978a) stated that the library community certainly could not "offer an alternative that gets politicians off the hook, allows them to stop supporting libraries with public funds by invoking user fees, then we'll surely have been guilty of that preemptive capitulation of which Shank spoke."

California's Attorney General Mr. Evelle J. Younger reminded the library community that charging fees for basic services was forbidden. The talk of fees was not unfounded. A survey revealed that by 1980, 40% of libraries instituted new fee structures (Berry, 1979b). This does not mean that these fees were for basics services.

The state librarian of California Ms. Ethel Crockett was vehemently opposed to the institution of fees. She explained that free library services were "as American as corn and Kansas and blueberry pie in the summer time. It's the reason we are strong as a nation" (White, 2011). The California Library Services Board was in concert with Ms. Crockett as they did not issue grants to any library that assessed fees, charged for services, or both.

Current ALA president Mr. Eric Moon spoke as well: "We should have launched already-and certainly should not delay beginning beyond this week – a massive effort, through ALA, through our chapters, through alliances with other associations and unions whose members and the services they supply are in similar jeopardy – an effort to inform and persuade the public of the full and disastrous consequences of their emotional response to ill-considered populist campaigns of this kind" (Berry et al., 1978).

Heading this call, a month later, the Tulsa City County Library System (Oklahoma) did in fact organize a massive effort to inform and persuade the public. Effectively using fund raising to back a campaign that included surveys, postcards, flyers, posters, yard signs, brochures, phone calls, bookmarks, public service announcements on television and radio, and full-page endorsement ads in newspapers. They engaged in conversation with many organizations, and received the backing of numerous Oklahoman celebrities in an effort to push back the Proposition 13 sentiment within the state and secure a $1 million increase in the budget.

American Library Association passed a resolution to begin communicating with Governor Brown, state legislatures, the California media, and the national

---

[14]LAPL had considered charging $5 per library card.

media (as they correctly suspected the tax revolt would spread to other areas of the country), calling attention to the effect this taxpayer revolt will have on libraries and that they stand for free and equal library service within California. They also agreed to form an ad hoc committee to investigate alternative means of public financing for libraries facing these budgetary crises.

Together the CLA and the CSL had petitioned the state legislature for 85% of their pre-Proposition 13 budgets. They believed that this percentage should be shared equally throughout the state and would help to maintain services equally throughout the state. If fulfilled, the request would help libraries to avoid charging fees and would maintain the acquisition of material. Further, the CLA stated that they would look for alternative funding for public libraries and believed that the 85% avoided irreparable damage to libraries. Their efforts were successful as the final number was 83% ("Californians Ask 85 Percent Funding for Libraries", *Library Journal*, 1978c).

After the proposition's passage, Governor Brown referred to himself as a "born-again tax cutter" (Walters, 2016). His stance of being against Proposition 13 before he was for Proposition 13 opened the door for critical assessment. State Assemblyman Mr. Paul Priolo referred to the governor as Jerry Jarvis, implying he was adopting the thoughts of Mr. Howard Jarvis. State Senator Peter Behr claimed the governor "shifts positions with such ease and good grace that you can't hear the clanking of the gears." Even Bob Hope couldn't resist a jab. Upon receiving a resolution to honor Mr. Hope on his 75th birthday, he joked he had "knocked on the door of the governor's mansion and Howard Jarvis answered" (Roberts, 2012).

It was reported that Mr. Hope did not amuse the governor.

However, the jokes and critiques did not slowdown Mr. Brown's 1978 reelection campaign for governor. He canvassed the state in part to explain how the proposition would not destroy those services Proposition 13's opponents feared it would. In fact, Mr. Brown's stance so impressed Mr. Jarvis that it moved him to make a television commercial for Mr. Brown's 1978 reelection efforts. The governor was reelected.

An interesting perspective of the climate within government came from Mr. Dennis Huey, who was the assistant auditor for Mendocino County. Shortly after passage, he attended a forum with other county and municipal officials in Sacramento regarding how to deal with the new law. Decades later, he would describe the government officials at the forum being "in tears" as Proposition 13 had broken a "lulled complacency" within the county government. It also eliminated approximately 100,000 public sector jobs, mostly from schools, and forced the closure of 75 branch libraries across the state (Bell, 2004).

Immediate Effect of Proposition 13

> *There will be no salary increases, possibly more state level "strings" attached to "bail out" money, and the 18 percent of the funds that were "carry over" from previous budgeting may not be available next year. – Librarian Mr. Clearance Walters (Berry, 1979b)*

The CLA also felt the effects of Proposition 13 both in their budget and at their annual conference, a four day event held December 2–5, 1978. Attendees meet to discuss the state of affairs in California libraries. That meant most of the discussion was regarding the impact of Proposition 13.

Reflecting a somber mood, the conference had fewer people attending, resulting in fewer events and fewer parties than were typical. Baker & Taylor donated the money ($1,500) they had earmarked for entertainment to the CLA to be used for any practical purpose.

The *Library Journal* (1979a) termed the annual conference the most depressing conference in CLA history. Disunity began to take hold. Those calling for a banding together or forming alliances were barely heard if listened to at all. This disunity was a manifestation of the fact that librarians were more concerned about their individual and/or local situation.

As they populated sessions on job-seeking, they spoke of looking for work outside the profession. Recent library school graduates fared no better. Given the scarcity of library jobs, they turned to employment such as landscaping, maid service, and secretarial work.

There were reports that some broke down physically and mentally because of the uncertainty and lost opportunities created by Proposition 13.

The CLA publication, *The California Librarian*, was suspended for as long as financial troubles persisted. Conference attendance was so sparse that constituent groups such as the California Society of Librarians and the California Institute of Libraries could not muster a quorum. This situation led the California Institute of Libraries to suggest that they dissolve, stating both a lack of purpose and program. Similarly, the last membership meeting of the CLA did not have the requisite minimum requirement of 200 members.

Contra Costa County Librarian Mr. Clarence Walters cut through the pall that hung over the conference, suggesting that another six months (essentially a year after passage) was needed before a proper assessment of Proposition 13 could be made.

No clear strategy would emerge from the chaos, panic, and disarray that had become the California library community. Conference attendees were at a loss as to how to work under conditions that included the following:

- Public libraries being opened for 10,877 fewer hours per week, a 22% reduction.
- Public library job losses totaling 1,228, a 21% reduction.
- Total public library income for operating expenses at 83% of the previous year.
- Funds for new materials being rolled back to 1975 levels, equaling a 20% reduction.
- A 50% reduction in interlibrary loan.
- The cutting back or elimination of services such as special programming for children and adults, as well as outreach to shut-ins and hospitals (Berry, 1979a; "Calif. Survey Pegs Impact of Proposition 13," *Library Journal*, 1979b).

The library community was hurt. The next question was how badly would libraries be hurt in the coming years? The predominant feeling throughout the conference was that things would only get worse. This sentiment was underscored by the State Finance Department alerting libraries to the disconcerting news that the state's bailout of $5.1 billion in 1978 would decrease in succeeding years to $4.5 billion in 1979 and $2.5 billion in 1980 (Berry, 1979a). This was due, in part, to other taxes not making up for the lost property tax revenue.[15]

Predictions were that it would take years to restore the services libraries were losing. What measures could be taken to mitigate the layoffs, reduced services, and budget cuts? Mr Clarence Walters and Mr David Sabsay were members of the CLA and served on Governor Brown's Committee on Government Reform. They were attempting to have the CLA's principles, dictated months after the proposition's passage, become law. As stated earlier the principles included; state funding of basic public library services, free access to library materials, a minimum of state control, and local administration of library services. Some in the CLA believed that all four of these principles contained in one piece of legislation might not be viable, although they do believe in the state providing funds. Others were quietly hoping for the state to buy out local public libraries.

As documented, the state initiated the $5.1 billion relief fund (Senate bill (SB) 154, providing approximately $4 billion in direct aid and $1 billion in emergency loan funds). It also assumed responsibility for $1 billion in mandates that were previously the onus of local, mostly county, governments. These steps, when combined with federal aid, budgetary surpluses, and slack resources in the system resulted in less than a 1% loss in total revenue to local government in the first year. Factored with a 7% increase in spending combined with a 10% inflation rate, real spending decreased for the fiscal year 1978–1979 (Danziger, 1980). This led local governments to cut library hours, reduce bus schedules, enact a 90% cancellation of summer school classes (Danziger, 1980), and reduce the public workforce. Additionally, many institutions, including libraries, began enacting user charges and other fees.

These action steps taken by local governments were either imperceptible for many citizens or judged as limited, and therefore confirmed the belief that local governments were bloated and could absorb a large tax cut. There was, as California Assembly Speaker Mr. Leo McCarthy stated, a pervasive "anti-government feeling-part of the tide of skepticism and cynicism" (Danziger, 1980) among the public.

Public service employment provided an uneasy feeling. The possibility of losing one's job, a less attractive financial situation, and a hostile political environment prompted some to retire voluntarily, and an expectation that qualified people will seek more stable industries in which to work. Further, minorities were hard hit by the reduction of available jobs as they had been using public service careers as a means of upward mobility.

---

[15]An Associated Press story indicated that the state distributed $5 billion a year for the first three years but was set to run out in June 1981.

When Governor Brown signed the billion dollar bailout,[16] he declared, "Proposition 13 creates challenges, it creates problems, but it creates an opportunity to make government in California a model for people all over the country" (*Time*, 1978d). In one sense he was correct regarding California becoming a role model for the country. In the immediate years subsequent to Proposition 13 Congress instituted numerous tax cuts.

The bailout (AKA Relief Fund) money was drawn from the state budget surplus that had increased to record levels during the 1970s and remained the record high until exceed in the late 1990s. This attempt to help local governments meant that the state was spending $1.5–2 billion more per year than it took in depleting the surplus by June 1981 (Willis, 1981).

Further, it was viewed as less effective for libraries than other public services as the law required only fire and police to be maintained at prior levels when bailout money was utilized. In other words, libraries were not high on the list of designated services. Although well meaning, this left health, social services, and libraries with a small piece of the bailout funds. Special District finances were severely affected because the state underestimated the amount of money they needed. Further complicating the issue for libraries within special district was the fact that they could not qualify for county funds, as it was viewed as a double taxation.

Governor Brown warned: "People who think there's a pot of gold in the state surplus are mistaken. They should not assume we are out of the woods" (Brodie, 1978). Mr. Jarvis had repeatedly stated that the state's budget surplus was much greater than the state would admit. To reiterate, the state found it hard to settle on a dollar figure for the surplus. Their initial estimate was $3 billion. That estimate was revised numerous times, moving as high as $6 billion. In 2009, there was a report that the state's surplus at the time Proposition 13 became law was $11 billion (Brodie, 1978; Citrin, 2009).

The relief funds came with mandates to local governments. They were to freeze wages of all employees for a year and maintain public safety functions at the same level as the previous year. Priority was given to emergency loan distribution, fire fighters, Medicaid, police, schools, and welfare.

Departments and services not given priority such as libraries, garbage collection, parks and recreation, public transportation, and street cleaning expected to experience deep cuts. A September 1978 survey conducted by the CSL and the CLA confirmed this expectation. Public libraries received little of the state's $4 billion relief fund. Survey respondents reported significant cuts in services, staffing, and buying power. In fact, only 8% of public library income came from state sources in the fiscal year 1978–1979 (*Library Journal*, 1979b).

Despite the grim news, libraries could find hope in public support. The ALA executive director Mr. Robert Wedgeworth pointed to the results of the

---

[16]Years later, some promulgated the thought that the state bailouts masked the consequences of the vote leading citizens to overstate the value of initiatives, thus passing more of them.

aforementioned *Los Angeles Times* poll that showed many more people agreeable to cutting welfare, parks, and recreation over libraries. However, a subdued tone persisted. As the *Library Journal* paused to reflect on the year 1978, it cautioned that celebratory might not be the proper word to sum up the year. Chief among the reasons to not blowing New Year's Eve horns were fiscal pressures on all types of libraries, inflation, and Proposition 13.

In some California cities, librarians did the work of library assistants and the assistants were laid off. Librarians complained that administrators were making these decisions without consulting them. Librarians, after all, were the closest to the day-to-day real-world ramifications of the new law and could serve as a resource for the best course of action. The *Journal of Academic Librarianship* (1978) ran an editorial suggesting some measures for librarians to consider. The measures were: pay more attention to community education programs, convince local authorities that vigorous library programs are essential, and selling (promote) libraries to their communities.

As public library budgets were written and rewritten,[17] predictions came raining down: fewer branches, shorter hours, elimination of all reference services, reduced book budgets, higher fines, and an increased number of service fees.

Librarians were asking for a close examination of the ramifications of budget cuts, with areas of concern being charging for services, using volunteers as replacement of library staff, the merging of libraries, the cost-effectiveness of interlibrary loan and non-print media services, the viability of age-level programs, and extension services. Nevertheless, libraries of all types went through a process of budget cuts, the effects of which ranged from damaging to draconian.

- Community Colleges, 50% supported by property taxes, were affected by the statewide hiring freeze. Naturally, there were no new positions being advertised, and some that were advertised prior to the passage of Proposition 13 were rescinded. Further, librarians saw their earning power reduced via a cut in hours.
- School libraries were given low priority. Shortly after the passage of the proposition no one knew what their status would be. What became clear through the budget cuts was the need for a reduction in library staff and a struggle to purchase materials.[18]
- The CSL planned a 10% budget cut and hiring freeze (Berry et al., 1978; Ousley-Swank, 2016; Plotnick, 1978).

The state university budget cuts were expected to be in the range of 10–15%. The university libraries adjusted their budgets accordingly. Most were not open in evenings or on the weekends through the summer months. Temporary help was laid off in June 1978 and vacant positions were left unfilled.

---

[17]The city of Livermore wrote seven budgets, Oakland and Los Angeles wrote six each.
[18]Coincidentally, school libraries were thrown into tumult in the very state that the School Library Section of the American Library Association held its first annual meeting. That occurred at the East Hall of the University of California on June 5, 1915.

The University of California (UC) experienced a dramatic budget cut in the academic year 1978–1979 when measured as a percentage of State's general fund. Higher education found good news in federal grants totaling $675,000 received by Stanford, the University of California at Berkeley (UC Berkley), and the UCLA to convert all new and retrospective serials not yet computerized into machine-readable form.

Actions Taken

It seemed for a while that county libraries in special districts would be spared, a bill, SB 2223, would have provided the needed money. However, the state's House attempted to add legislation that would increase aid to welfare recipients. Upon seeing this, the state's Senate nixed the bill, leading to its demise.

The sum of SB 2223 failing, Proposition 13 passing, and the bailout dictate that its money keep fire and police at prior funding levels meant libraries within special districts faced bad, some said devastatingly bad, news regarding funding:

- Palo Verdes had a 60% reduction in hours, 54% reduction in acquisition funding, 58% reduction in staff, and a $1 million debt.
- Tulare received a 65% budget cut.
- Yolo experienced a 62% budget cut (*Library Journal*, 1978d; White, 2011).

Despite the federal contribution to California state libraries increasing by $1,113,262, the CSL expected a 10% budget cut and braced for the hiring freeze. The state's contribution to local libraries increased by $13,497,220 yet still left a budgetary shortfall of $35 million. Cities sought to save budgets by raising taxes. This act follows the supposition that Proposition 13 was not a tax windfall, rather a budget balance shift from the property tax to the income tax.

A survey sponsored by the CSL and the Californian Library Association published in December 1978 found that 28 libraries serving 2.9 million people received a 1978–1979 budget increase, while 28 libraries serving 4.5 million people received budgets of less than 70% of the previous year. Thirty-nine libraries serving roughly 6 million people fell within a range of 70–85% of last year's budget, while 46 libraries serving roughly 7.6 million people received budgets within a range of 86–100% of the previous year's budget (Berry, 1979b).

In total, the operating income for all public libraries declined by $35,285,976 and the local income for public libraries declined by $49,896,458. These declines negated some of the hoped for positive effects coming from the state bailout (Berry, 1979a).

The Alameda County Library, heavily reliant on property taxes for funding, closed 13 libraries for a month and laid off 245 library workers. Twelve employees were retained to process the mail, maintain the holdings, and manage other operations. This was a decision made by the board of supervisors 17 days after Proposition 13 was passed. The 13 Alameda County libraries were closed beginning on June 26, 1978. Three remained closed while 10 were eventually opened on a limited basis. They operated with fewer hours and cut or eliminated their services and programs. In a unique twist to raise money, Alameda County librarian Ms. Elizabeth Talbot held a raffle to guess the date for what would happen first – the construction of a new branch or the removal of her braces. Construction did continue for two library buildings. Those furloughed included 20-year employees and some employees nearing retirement. The library system worked at 36% of the previous year's budget. The board of supervisors did not grant money from the general fund. There was doubt of getting beyond 50% of their former level of service. On September 3, 1978, the library began the process of hiring back both aides and librarians. An October 1978 *Library Journal* (1978e) article noted that by September 11, 1978 the library system had returned to 80% of the previous budget level for the next 10 months. However, the *Library Journal* (1978d) also mentioned that staff cuts were 71% equaling 177 people let go leaving 71 still employed. They were not taking requests for specific books. A little more than four months hence the passage of the proposition, there were no age-specific specialist on staff and they had limited the children and young adult programs. Library employees organized a coalition titled Coalition to Restore Quality Library Service. It was designed to inform the public about the effects of the budget cuts. They were helped in protest by friends of the library that included residents and authors. The coalition spent the Summer and Fall selling cartoon "Jarvis Canned" t-shirts, handing out leaflets, protesting at council meetings, lobbying in Sacramento, and forming alliances with other library groups, booksellers, authors, unions, and writers. They resisted in actions and in words; Alameda County Librarian Ms. Barbara Boyd at first refused to close down the system stating, "I never thought I'd see the day. Libraries have never been closed during wars or floods or anything" (White, 2011). By November, reports stated, the libraries were open for half their previous hours with the above-mentioned staff cuts only after less than pleasant meetings occurred between the public and the county board of supervisors. Librarian Ms. Ginnie Cooper who would later be Library Director at the Multnomah County Library, Portland when they too were in the middle of a tax revolt, commentated on a new library skill: "We have had to become political. It's now as important as knowing how to catalogue" (White, 2011).

In other developments across the state.

- Benicia Public Library relied on volunteers to provide extra community services.
- Grassroots efforts were begun. In Carpinteria, the Friends of the Carpinteria Library helped the town's people contact their county supervisor. They addressed envelopes in the names of the supervisors and then held meetings to distribute those envelopes. Carpinteria lost 35% of its budget and some of its hours. The grassroots efforts were credited with keeping the budget cut to no worse than 35%.
- Colton Public Library was aided by the city government making "cuts from behind the scenes activities" to other government services. These cuts ensured the library was fully funded.

The ramifications of the inaction regarding SB 2223 could be demonstrated at the Contra Costa County library. County Librarian Mr. Clarence Walters noted that the county will now need to decide whether it should dip into the general fund to meet its monetary obligations to the police and fire departments. If that was necessary, the money taken from the general fund would be that which is typically allocated to the county library, resulting in a 65% budget cut.

As it turned out, the Contra Costa Public Library received a budget for 1978–1979 nearly equal to the previous year. Still, as Mr. Walters explained, during the first year of Proposition 13 the library experienced, "less staff, less maintenance, less buying power and a significant reduction in … its service capability" ("Balancing the Budget in Contra Costa Calif." *Library Journal*, 1979g). The focus was on keeping public services in place while making cuts in non-public administrative and technical support service activities. To balance the budget, nine permanent library staff positions were eliminated, the materials budget was reduced by 8%, maintenance hours were reduced, and funds for furniture and equipment, committee functions, and library programs were eliminated.

A deeper look into Contra Costa's personnel issues saw a consolidation within children services and acquisitions along with a streamlining of the hiring process of student assistants accompanied by a reduction in the working hours of student assistants. The goal of this streamlining was to use the students in place of library professionals. Complicating personnel issues was the board of supervisors reversing its decision to hire for positions at a new library branch for fear of having to lay them off in the next fiscal year. Instead, they reassigned existing personnel. Due to these reductions and reassignments, the library was not able to maintain former levels of service. Response time to patrons' request went up and programs for adults and children went down.

The library looked to automation as a cost-saving measure becoming one of the first in California to join a pilot project using Baker and Taylor's online book-ordering system. Additionally, they decided to transition to the Research Libraries Information Network (RLIN) online catalog. Other actions that were taken included the cessation of purchasing high-priced reference materials and periodicals, purchasing paperback copies instead of hard copies, and severely cutting the purchase of audio-visual material.

Looking ahead, Mr. Walters was asked to submit budgets at 100%, 95% and 90% of funding (*Library Journal*, 1979g). He hoped for the same budget as 1978. However, given inflation and salary increase, this would be the equivalent of a 16–20% budget cut (*Library Journal*, 1979g). Mr. Walters admitted that public service would have to share in any cuts, favoring that over reducing library programs. He expressed hope that the state could resolve its long-term financing problems to local government. In the meantime, he prepared for budget cuts of as high as 10% ("Contra Costa Budget Inches Up 1.5%," *Library Journal*, 1979i). These preparations included cutting 18 permanent positions, further reductions in library student hours, a countywide reduction in operating hours per week totaling 144 hours, and a 19% reduction in the acquisitions budget. Within the acquisitions budget was a projected book budget of $467,000. This was down from the 1977–1978 level of $638,000. Further, there was a volumes purchased drop to 55,000 from 86,000. ("Balancing the budget in Contra Costa, Calif." 1979).

In 1979, it was reported that the Contra Costa Library System would receive an incremental budgetary increase of 1.5% for the next fiscal year (*Library Journal*, 1979i). This was rather good news, as Mr. Walters had feared a decrease in the range of 5–10% (*Library Journal*, 1979i). He commented that Contra Costa "fared better than a great many other California libraries affected by Proposition 13 linked reductions in tax support." They were able to fill four vacancies, yet had to freeze 18 positions and reduce the acquisitions budget by 22% or $110,000 of a $500,000 budget within which the book budget was cut by $30,000. The acquisitions budget money was reallocated to pay outstanding obligations to book dealers (*Library Journal*, 1979i).

Corona Public Library experienced an $11,000 budget decrease ("More on Proposition 13: Book Cuts & Frozen Salaries," *Library Journal*, 1978g). Rather than reducing hours or staff, they decided to cut the book budget, freeze staff salaries, impose fees on both the use of meeting rooms and the interlibrary loan borrowing of microfilm. They raised overdue fines and employed (through the Comprehensive Employment and Training Act, CETA) a husband and wife team to track down overdue books. However, instead of collecting fines, the couple accepted donations (*Library Journal*, 1978g).

The Coronado Public Library suffered through a 50% cut in its budget, resulting in a reduction in the hours of operation, leaving it open for a scant three days per week (White, 2011).

Daly City Public Library received a 57% budget cut (*Library Journal*, 1978d).

In the East Bay (San Francisco area), interlibrary loan for books was stopped ("Jarvis Hits the Bay Area," *Library Journal*, 1978e).

Hayward Public Library (Alameda County) maintained 95% of its budget, was not expected to cut staff or services; however, they were expected to charge fees of non-residents (Plotnick, 1978).

Huntington Beach Public Library was able to raise taxes, ensuring $1 million per annum for the library. Ahead of their time, they instituted food service within the library as a means of making money. For a short while, they charged admission to a popular children's story time and instituted a fee for new library cards (White, 2011).

The Irvine Public Library reconfigured its construction plans, dropping to a 10,000^2 feet facility from the original plan of 30,000^2 feet (White, 2011).

The Livermore Public Library budget was cut by 36%, resulting in a loss of staff (Plotnick, 1978), charging non-residents as much as $40 per family, (White, 2011), reducing hours of operation, cutting children services (*Library Journal*, 1978d), and scrapping plans for a new library (Plotnick, 1978).

The Los Gatos Public Library (Santa Clara County) began charging non-residents $25 (*Library Journal*, 1978e).

Marin County Free Library staff was cut from 55.5 to 38.5 (*Library Journal*, 1978e).

In Monrovia, California, there was a 10.27% cut of city's 185 employees, including four of the six librarians. The city manager, Mr. Robert R. Ovrom stated: "Jarvis said that his measure would mean a 10% cut in local budgets. Here it's more like 30%. But we'll just have to make it work" (*Time*, 1978c).

Palo Verdes, as did many public libraries, turned to volunteers. Yet, Palo Verdes went one-step further than simply asking the public to volunteer. They asked the public to donate a portion of the money saved in property taxes to the library (*Time*, 1978c; White, 2011).

Pomona City library suffered cuts of 50% in both its full-time staff and book acquisitions budget and a 75% cut in its audiovisual acquisitions budget (White, 2011).

Richmond's Public Library budget was cut by 65% (Plotnick, 1978). All Librarian I's and II's were laid off. The total staff was down by 17 people and its acquisitions budget dropped by 87% from $120,000 to $16,000 (*Library Journal*, 1978e).

Los Angeles County had begun preparations for Proposition 13's passage nearly two months before it was voted on, in April, by ordering a freeze on hiring and promotions. Immediately after the proposition was passed, the county announced that firemen, hospital workers, and sheriff's deputies would be among the 37,000 county employees to be laid off. At the time, the county employed 73,000 people (*Facts on File World News Digest*, 1978). One laid-off county employee was enrolled at Los Angeles Trade-Technical College (Trade Tech) to become a locksmith. Mr. Scott Bryan was eventually hired back by the city in his new occupation and interestingly found himself working on library locks.

The city of Los Angeles announced that 1,080 police will be a part of the 8,300 city employees to be laid off. At the time, the city employed 29,000 people (*Facts on File World News Digest*, 1978).

Once Proposition 13 was passed, LAPL immediately began strategizing to keep the budget cut between 15% and 20%, a project that library director Mr. Wyman Jones called "miraculous." Within this process they crafted six contingency budgets. A 15–20% budget reduction would fare well against the backdrop of the 60% budget cuts forecasted in nearby counties. The final budget cut was 10%, thanks to $70 million coming from the state's surplus bailout. Still, it was not easy to digest. Mr. John Holleman, a branch librarian, lamented, "No more programming, no more outreach to the nine area schools we've been involved with" (Plotnick, 1978).

The Los Angeles City Council felt the lobbying efforts from the airport workers, courts, fire department, hospitals, and police. The library relied on friends and grassroots citizen support to lobby the LA City Council. City Hall received as many letters about library service as it did for the police. In support of the library, people started picketing in front of the Pacoima Branch in the San Fernando Valley.

Picketing signs in both Spanish and English read as such:

- Cut city hall fat.
- Give me libraries or give me death.

- Prop 13 means minority persecution.
- Save our kids.

The LAPL Library Guild took a stance that it would be intolerable to accept salary cuts in lieu of layoffs. It was expected that the most recent to be hired will be the first to be fired. Many of the most recent to be hired were to serve minority communities.

In the end, the LA City Council issued a statement regarding LAPL, ordering salary reduction of 10% through attrition and no layoffs. Four libraries were closed and the city took back the $43 million renovation project for LAPL's central library, suggesting that they find alternate funding for the renovation (Plotnick, 1978).

Reducing budgets locally also had an effect on the support being provided by the federal government. The CETA program (comprising full-time workers) and other grants were based on the "maintenance of local effort." For LAPL, as many as 71 CETA-related jobs were in jeopardy of being eliminated.

Another complication related to the myriad budgetary issues was that vendors were reticent to do business with Los Angeles until their financial situation stabilized.

A surprise move came in August. The city performed a budgetary course reversal as it prepared a budget that was $200 million more than that of the previous year (Brodie, 1978). Credit for this new direction was given to the funds received via the state surplus.

Though the poor were expected to see a reduction in services, it is important to note that this isn't a situation where the rich were to go unscathed. Budget cuts were frequently based on the proportion of money the community received via the property tax. Meaning that, the local government of an affluent community may receive more of its revenue from the property tax than a poorer community, and therefore had to enact larger cuts in public services. At the Redondo Beach Public Library – the Redondo Beach communities are some of the most expensive in the United States – the head librarian was demoted to head of reference, and the rest of the professional staff were fired. Pages were spared to help in circulation.

The state surplus was instrumental in helping Riverside City and County Library keep all twenty-one branches open and rehire fourteen people originally laid off. On the downside, branch hours were cut as was the book budget, sharply, from $220,436 to $75,000 (*Library Journal*, 1978g). Palm Springs Public Library (located within Riverside County) experienced a unique situation. The loss of funding forced two of their four libraries to be put up for sale to help ensure financial stability. Simultaneous to that they received a 56% increase to the acquisition budget (from $36,000 to $56,000) and the money needed to connect to the Online Computer Library Center (OCLC). Library Director Mr. Henry Weiss attributed the acquisitions budget increase to long-range community planning as opposed to simply asking for more money. He explained, "You are in a much better position to argue for book money if you go to the trouble of pinning down the acquisition needs of your community and putting this data in a formal presentation" ("Palm Springs Ups Book $$ Despite Proposition 13," *Library Journal*, 1979c).

Sacramento lost 23% of their budget in the first year and a possible 33% additional in the second year. The initial 23% cut resulted in a reduction of 300 hours in service, many branches were closed on Saturdays, book purchases were reduced, the McNaughton book rental plan was cancelled, film rentals were terminated, overdue fines were raised, and a combined 256 full-time, part-time, on call, and substitute employees were laid off ("Sacramento Faces Threats of Devastating $$ Cuts," *Library Journal*, 1979d). Sacramento library director Mr. Harold Martelle explained that if the 33% cut were to be enacted, additional service hours might be cut, a further reduction in the book budget was possible, branches might be paired or closed, more staff might have to be let go, and more fees for service would be considered.

Proposition 13 demonstrated the need for librarians to inform both the government and the citizenry about the value of a library within the community and by contrast what could happen if libraries became less of a priority. In other words, librarian's needed to advocate for themselves as they never had before.

To that end, approximately 300 Sacramentans, with the library director in attendance, rallied to support the library at a town hall meeting that was focused on budgetary matters. Addressing the town hall gathering with regard to the possible 33% budget cut, library director Mr. Martelle stated: "If the library is to endure such a cut, the Sacramento Public Library, for all intents and purposes will cease to exist as a library."

He asked the crowd to put pressure on local government for aid, join the Friends, and volunteer at their branch library. Putting it succinctly, Mr. Martelle stated, "If you want quality library services then you will have to get out and lobby for them." He also pointed to the fact that the library budget cut was "larger than any endured by other city or county departments." He promised a series of town hall meetings "to provide a forum for the exchange of information between the library and its consumers" (*Library Journal*, 1979d).

The Salinas Public Library stopped providing telephone reference to save $15,000. The money saved allowed for two branch libraries to remain open.

The city of San Diego came under fire for cutting their library budget by 16%. That was slightly more than three times the average 5% budget cut received by other San Diego departments. Yet the library accounted for only 2% of the city's budget. This cut forced the San Diego Public Library to reduce hours, temporarily close branches, end the cataloging of government documents, and to begin charging fees for new library cards. On the plus side; at a time when many libraries did not or could not, San Diego managed to hold onto its acquisition budget.

The City of San Diego budget cuts shook up employment. Sixty-nine out of 286 (24%) library positions were eliminated. Twenty-nine of the first 32 immediate city layoffs were librarians, 22 combined senior librarian and supervisory positions were eliminated, the same number was cut from youth services, and

39 librarians were demoted – 17 of these from professional to paraprofessional positions[19] (Berry, 1979b). It was reported that these demotions were voted on by a city council that felt the pressure of Mayor Pete Wilson's office to do so. The CLA went on record as being opposed to these actions, while the ALA sent a representative to the city hearings to testify against the demotions.

A confounding issue was that the City of San Diego sat on $16 million in unallocated funds. To be fair, the city leaders might have been saving these funds as an emergency hedge, since most within the state did not have a clear expectation as to what the state budget would look like in the coming years. Many saw the library budget cuts as a bit of revenge for an equal opportunity complaint filed against the city by librarians in 1977 for unequal treatment given to males over female employees.

The city and county of San Francisco retained 99% of its budget, thus avoiding the unpleasantness of library closing (Brodie, 1978).

The City of San Leandro Public Library (Alameda County) maintained 80% of its budget, expected no cuts to staff, scheduled a phasing out of four of the five branches, dropped out of the California Film Circuit, and began to charge fees with the thought that a worse budget in 1979 may be in the offing.

San Mateo County was able to keep normal operating hours and maintained basic services. However, to help facilitate this, there was a staff cut from 170 to 88, and they began charging for audio-visual services (*Library Journal*, 1978b, 1978d).

Solano County library staff were cut from 313 to 45 (*Library Journal*, 1978d).

In the Ventura County library system, a 22% budget cut lead to the elimination of 37 of the 128 staff positions. To keep the system functioning, Ventura County leaned heavily on volunteers. In fact, a special volunteer training program designed to provide staff to extend hours at some of the smaller branches resulted in five communities experiencing an increase in their library service of 26 hours. Other volunteers were trained in areas that included book mending, circulation assistants, film programmers, gardening, shelving, and storytelling. The first six months of the program saw 162 people volunteering a total of 6,189 hours or $25,499 if based on the pay rate for a clerical worker ("Proposition 13 Spurs Use of Volunteers in Ventura," *Library Journal*, 1979e).

Similar to the Corona Public Library using a husband and wife to collect overdue library books, although certainly not as neighborly, other California libraries had utilized collection agencies to gather missing resources such as lost, overdue, and stolen books.

It was effective:

- Altadena brought back half of its missing resources.
- Covina reduced missing books from 900 to 300 per year.
- Huntington Beach effectively combined a collection agency and staffer to bring losses down from $30,000 to $2,000 in one year.
- Pomona recouped $2,000 in losses per month.

---

[19]Throughout California library administrators were also demoted leaving those they moved out as jobless.

For a year, the state budget surplus helped libraries of all types survive the aftermath of Proposition 13. Beyond that, libraries needed to strategize, as it was known that the state's surplus was not going to last forever.[20] This strategy included a persistent effort to persuade legislatures, supervisors, and city councilors to support libraries. The legislatures, in particular those serving on the Proposition 13 committee, spent as much as 15 hours a day sorting out the state surplus and establishing priorities.

Grassroots efforts continued in the support of libraries. Many library coalitions fought for the $4.7 million available through the California Library Services Act.

The Oakland Public Library received support from the neighborhood community, businesses, and the city council. Ms. Mary Moore, a member of the Oakland City Council, opined regarding the budget cuts: "It's like asking whether you want your left leg or your right leg" (Plotnick, 1978). A decision the Oakland Public Library did not have to make as they received an increase in funding due in part to the leadership of the library director and a new tax.

Hope was found in the continued lobbying by organizations such as the state's library unions and the Bay Area's Coalition to Restore Quality Library Services, especially in Los Angeles, San Francisco, San Jose, and Palo Alto. These efforts had some impact on politicians and the citizens. However, there was not a broad based groundswell to unite other municipal workers and citizens that would have been needed to turn back Proposition 13.

An initial peek into next year did not show optimism for what lay ahead. With governments continuing to cut expenses, library decision makers were once again considering raising user fees (at the CLA annual conference in December 1978, one library director gave an impassioned plea for the justification of user fees), initiating layoffs, seeking volunteers, replacing professionals with lower-salaried paraprofessionals, combining libraries from different jurisdictions, cutting services (with a fear that services to minorities would be most jeopardized), and branch closings.

However, in 1979, Governor Brown signed into law AB 8. This legislation was in essence a tax shift. Taking property tax revenue that typically went to schools and shifting it to cities, counties, and special districts to use as they saw fit. In its stead, the school districts received cash payments from the state. AB 8 left cities and counties in a fairly good position for 1979. Cities received a total of $207 million, that amount was equal to their 1978–1979 property tax allocation. Additionally, cities received 83% of their 1978–1979 block grant money. Counties received a total of $312 million, an amount that was equal to their 1978–1979 property tax allocation. Counties also received 100% of their 1978–1979 block grant money (Calif. Okays Long-Range $$ measures to Aid Localities, *Library Journal*, 1979h).

Contra Costa County Librarian Mr. Clarence Walters explained that cities fared worse in the 1979 state aid distribution. The reason was that cities were less reliant on property tax revenue as other jurisdictions and had a greater ability to raise other sources of revenue. Not that cities and libraries will do poorly. Rather, Mr. Walters judged that cities and libraries will still do well. Exceptions would be libraries that were ranked by their city government near the bottom of the priority list such as Daly City and Richmond.

---

[20]The state surplus lasted until fiscal year 1981–1982.

Still, AB 8 was not a panacea for all the ills faced by libraries. It did not provide the money necessary for libraries to keep up with inflation nor replace all of the funding lost with the reductions in tax support that were a result of Proposition 13. Mr. Walters commented that libraries will have to fight for their share of the tax funds made available under AB 8 as they had to when last year's bail out money was provided.

What did AB 8 provide? "Long range funding for local jurisdictions," Mr. Walters explained, "but (it) does not single out libraries or any other public service for special consideration" (*Library Journal*, 1979h). Legislatures claimed that making libraries a priority at the expense of other Proposition 13 service cutbacks, such as health and welfare, would force those other services to seek priority status. If that were to happen, the legislatures feared, the bill would not have passed.

On the plus side: Under AB 8, local jurisdictions will have more flexibility to spend the money as they see fit. This, the library community hoped, would make it easier to obtain the funds. Interestingly, AB 8 allowed county free libraries that were considered special districts to be eligible for both special district funds and county funds.

Two positive developments occurred that led to an increase in tax revenue. There was a 2% growth rate in tax levels combined with new money coming in from reassessments when there was a change in property ownership. The CLA estimated that these two occurrences would lead to a 10% statewide increase in tax revenue.

Further, people were optimistic that another bill, SB 958, was gaining support in the California legislature. This bill would allocate $157 million in state aid to public libraries (*Library Journal*, 1979h). Mr. Walters believed that direct state aid to libraries was required, and if AB 8 did not adequately fund public libraries, SB 958 will be revived (*Library Journal*, 1979h). He was of the opinion that the finalized number for SB 958 will be less than the $157 million initially proposed; however, he viewed any state aid to libraries as a significant breakthrough. It was estimated that the failure to pass this legislation would cost libraries approximately 25% of their current budgets (Berry, 1980). Mr. Waters was correct in the fact that the bill was pared down. The initial bill had a per capita cost of $11. Upon arriving on Governor Brown's desk, in 1980, that cost was $1 per capita. It was still too much for the state budget as Governor Brown vetoed the bill and explained that the state's financial instability necessitated the veto ("Brown Nixes State Aid to California Libraries," *Library Journal*, 1980d).

What Happens Next?

We are now in the second year of our great conservative revolt … and public libraries are directly in the line of fire. The revolt is, in fact, a revolt against public services for the less fortunate and poor … it rests firmly on the dislike for paying taxes.
– Harvard Economist, Mr. John Kenneth Gailbraith (Berry, 1979a)

As the chaos of Proposition 13's passage began to ebb, one could find two types of Californians. Those who were happy to have their taxes cut and others who feared for the survival of public services. Evidence of how pleased citizens were with Proposition 13 was seen in the passing of Mr. Paul Gann's Proposition 4, *The Gann Limit Initiative*. It passed on November 6, 1979, 16 months after Proposition 13, with 74.3% of the voters approving. Colloquially known as the "Spirit of 13," this proposition limited state and local government spending to the increase in the cost of living adjusted for population growth. (Both are based on percentage increases.) For a jurisdiction to exceed this limit would require approval from a majority of voters. It required both state and local governments to provide a rebate to taxpayers of any money collected in excess of the limitation for any fiscal year, and for the state to repay the local government for the cost of compliance with state mandates ("California's Proposition 4, the Gann Limit Initiative 1979", Ballotpedia, n.d.; Son of Proposition 13, 1979).

Unlike Proposition 13, there was little debate and less emotion surrounding Proposition 4. Public officials, including Governor Jerry Brown, were reticent to openly oppose it. The combined effect of inflation raising real estate prices (three years into Proposition 13, property values were still increasing rapidly, leading to higher reassessments, resulting in greater than anticipated governmental revenue), the bailout via the state's budget surplus, and an increase in user fees had lessened the effects of Proposition 13. This lessening was thought to be a contributing factor to the ease by which Proposition 4 was passed. Despite the fear that more control would be handed over to the state, it passed with more support than Proposition 13: 2,580,720 people having voted for Proposition 4, while 891,157 people voted against (Ballotpedia, n.d.) with a ratio of 2.9:1.

Despite a loophole,[21] it was still considered a more restrictive proposition than Proposition 13. By the mid-1980s, it bore more responsibility for a reduction in public services than Proposition 13. There were two factors that made this as such. Firstly, the citizens' demands for the state's public services (specifically jails, roads, and schools) were exceeding Proposition 4's funding metric. Second, on many occasions Governor Deukmejian's interpretation of the proposition led to the enactment of the clause that compelled refunds to the citizens. Given Proposition 4's tenets, rising inflation occasionally offered the opportunity for modest increases in funding for public services. Until 1986, that is, when the measures within Proposition 4 leaned on California's budgets as inflation dipped, possibly resulting in state and local governments again refunding money to taxpayers. Simultaneous to this occurrence, reports surfaced of a budget threat to libraries and other public services.

Any law that limits government spending may spiral down to public services in a negative manner. Public libraries were still adjusting to the new reality of these two tax and spending limits passed into law in two successive years (1978 and

---

[21]The money restricted was money allocated to general fund expenditures. Government simply would move money out of the general fund.

1979). They reacted quickly with plans that resulted in deep cuts in programs, budgets, and personnel, yet kept the doors open as best as they could.

The *Library Journal*, covering the 1979 American Libraries Annual Conference in Dallas, termed Harvard economist Mr. John Kenneth Gailbraith's address "a stirring indictment of the underlying views of the tax revolt" (Berry, 1979a). Mr. Gailbraith stated, "We are now in the second year of our great conservative revolt ... and public libraries are directly in the line of fire. The revolt is, in fact, a revolt against public services for the less fortunate and poor[22] ... it rests firmly on the dislike for paying taxes" (Berry, 1979a).

Mr. Gailbraith went on to point out that two-thirds of the tax savings benefited corporations or large property owners, while diminished services had their heaviest impact on those representing the lowest income brackets. He urged public employees to "shake off the habit of passive neutrality on public issues" (Berry, 1979a) and laid out the following six rules to be guided by as follows:

- A stronger response to attacks made on public service.
- Increased action and political sophistication is needed to change current methods of dealing with inflation (monetary and fiscal policy).
- Large and regular relocation of federal funds for local uses.
- Many of the essential services of society must be decided upon collectively.
- Professional pride leading to a stronger, self-confident defense of public services.
- Public employees have to be more efficient than private employees (Berry, 1979b).

Others were more neutral than Mr. Gailbraith, with a general feeling that Proposition 13 had not lived up to the supporters' hopes or the foes' worries. As mentioned previously, Proposition 13's financial hardship was mitigated by the state bailout. Further relief came in the form of an increase in sales-tax revenue that was created by a consumer spending binge, which found its origins in the money consumers saved via Proposition 13. Local government spending increases were below both inflation and increases of the recent past. A survey of 6,300 local budgets surprisingly found an average increase of 1.1% over 1977–1978 levels. However, that pales when compared with the heretofore 1970's average annual increase of 10.5% (Lawrence, 1979). Still, it was reported that local governments wound up receiving 96% of the revenue that had been expected.

> Our argument will be that any government collection of money
> is a tax.
> – Mr. Howard Jarvis (Bonventre, Kasindorf, & Reese, 1979)

Government institutions, including libraries, looked to the initiation of fees as a revenue source. LA County imposed admission fees at museums and gardens

---

[22]Decades later, columnist Mr. Peter Schrag defined the reduction in public services as hurting new Californian immigrants and their children.

and raised parking fees at county beaches. Across the state fees were raised for services such as garbage collection, summer school, and permits. Parking meters, many would argue a hidden tax, were installed and youth sports programs were being charged for the use of public parks. In addition to the institution of charges and fees, citizens donated hundreds of thousands of dollars to help stabilize budgets for schools, parks, and other items of concern.

One year into Proposition 13, the average homeowner was still coming out ahead, however, there was concern about the increased prevalence of fees and that they might become as burdensome as the property tax used to be. Many perceived the initiation of fees as a means to avoid Proposition 13's requirement of a two-thirds voter approval for new taxes. Mr. Jarvis joined several of the lawsuits that were filed to stop this practice.

The fees hurt attendance. The Los Angeles County Museum of Art reported a 50% decrease in patronage while the Los Angeles County Arboretum and Botanic Garden, as well as other museums, reported similar declines.

The cuts felt by libraries, state-financed recreation programs, some school systems, and many state and local government jobs seemed to exact their toll mostly on the poor, the elderly, and the young. Examples abound, such as welfare recipient Ms. Debra Walker. She and her son faced eviction because there was no cost-of-living increase for those on welfare. As Ms. Walker stated: "It was a matter of eating and not paying my rent. So now I am getting evicted" (Lawrence, 1979)

Youths were effected not by losing a job, but by not getting a job. Vacancies, some by retirement, that went unfilled were originally to be filled by those in the younger age bracket of the workforce.

The state and local government workforce experienced a reduction of 100,000 jobs, from 1.52 million to 1.42 million employed (Lawrence, 1979). (Note that another report indicated the job loss for public employment to be 120,000.) Neither fire nor police departments experienced significant cuts in budgets or in personnel. Lessening the severity of the jobs lost is the fact that 83,200 of the 100,000 jobs were either resignations or retirements. Additionally, many of those who resigned or retired from a public job did find work in the 500,000 jobs that were created by California's strong private sector job market.

To be sure, a talent drain did occur from the public workforce. One year after the propositions' passage state librarian Ms. Ethel Crockett wrote that there was, "a rash of early retirements of highly competent librarians and the sudden dismissal of library directors who had received no previous hint of unsatisfactory performance...Some of California's best librarians are looking for positions in other fields, and some have found them. Fewer out of state librarians are seeking positions in California so not as much new talent is enriching the state" (*Library Journal*, 1979h).

Contra Costa County Librarian Mr. Clarence Walters echoed Ms. Crockett, "California is losing many of its top notch librarians, who are going into other fields or moving on to other states" (*Library Journal*, 1979i).

Ms. Crockett also addressed the lack of revenue inevitably becoming a major catalyst for change starting with librarians who will be forced to "think through alternative ways of providing library service" (*Library Journal*, 1979h).

Further, librarians will be replaced by technicians and clerical assistants. Support staff would be expected to take responsibility for more of the "librarian work" (*Library Journal*, 1979h) as the number of professional positions was reduced. And those librarians who remained "may either do everything, including clerical work, or will have the opportunity to concentrate on very high caliber professional work" (*Library Journal*, 1979h).

Mixed within all the news regarding budget reductions were reports of community engagement, business support, and library activism.

The Chula Vista school district created Proposition Plus Night. It was an effort to raise money for the Chula Vista Public Library's children department. The money raised would be used for the purchase of books and materials. It was a talent show with singers, dancers, a barbershop quartet, and a 25-piece band. Many of the performers were students and teachers. There was food and soft drink stands. A San Diego radio personality served as the mistress of ceremonies. An auction was held with one featured item being a San Diego Chargers signed football. One could browse the mini-book sale run by the Library Friends or dine with top city officials and the superintendent of schools. After expenses, they raised over $1,000. City Librarian Mr. Bradley Simon commented, "It was a thoughtful and popular gesture on the part of our local teachers and was more successful than any of us had hoped for ... we are looking forward to the second annual Proposition Plus Night."

The Kern County Library had survived the Proposition 13 aftermath and two years hence had made a "very substantial and rapid comeback" according to County Librarian Mr. Robert Cannon. To wit, 24 new positions, 11 of those being professional will be opened. The materials budget has been fully restored, hours will be increased for all major facilities, and there is increased money for training and delivery. Mr. Cannon went on to say that thanks to the help of volunteers, laid off volunteers, the flexibility of the staff, and the juggling of personnel, duties, assignments, and funds, "we made it through an unparalleled period of crises ... we look forward ... to brighter, creative, and more productive periods ahead" ("Kern Co Makes Comeback," *Library Journal*, 1979j).

The San Bernardino Public Library saw a 10% overall budget increase in the second year of Proposition 13. That included 15% more for books and the funding for a $7,500^2$ feet branch library built primarily for the Mexican–American community. To ensure construction of the new branch, the San Bernardino Public Library initiated a lobbying effort focusing on both the city government and the city's citizens. Their efforts included proving that there had been an increase in the funding base – by 60% from grants and volunteer services – and their expenditures would remain flat because they would be closing two inferior branches in conjunction with the opening of the new branch library. Librarian Mr. Stephen Whitney commented that the library was helped by common cause shared between librarians and politicians. Specifically, a "growing interest in meeting the needs of California's minorities and disadvantaged that appeals to politicians and librarians, too." The results of a door-to-door survey illustrating citizens concern for libraries was submitted to the town. Another item that helped the library's cause was a children's summer reading program that was so successful the schools noticed the improvement in students reading that fall. Not to be overlooked, the summer reading program also raised circulation by 200% ("San Bernardino $$ Up, Chicanos, a service Priority," *Library Journal*, 1979k).

The Santa Fe City Library was not affected by Proposition 13 and, in fact, stated that they came out ahead. They also were benefactors of the Powerine Oil Company who underwrote a monthly showing of children's feature films, and a donation from author Mr. Irving Stone for a local historic program to include photographic murals. Mr. Stone's donation came after the library had dedicated its building expansion to him.

The actions taken in the immediate aftermath of Proposition 13 were in response to the new tax law leading to the reformation of government financing, plus California's economic condition. Financial experts believed that if left unchanged, state taxes were strong enough to provide proper aid to local governments. Supporters of Proposition 13, no doubt buoyed by victory, continued the initiation of new proposals to restrict taxes and government spending. This included Mr. Gann and Mr. Jarvis, but with a twist. The duo had broken up for their encores to Proposition 13. As mentioned, Mr. Gann's Proposition 4, a formula-based limit on government spending, was successful at the polls. Mr. Jarvis' initiative was a state constitutional amendment known as Proposition 9 or Jaws II. The aim was to cut state income tax in half, totaling $3 billion in tax savings. Regarding Proposition 9, state treasurer Mr. Jesse Unruh said, "If that passes we have a whole different ball game. It's back to square one" (Bonventre, Kasindorf, & Reese, 1979). The year 1980 will show if Mr. Jarvis's Proposition 9 achieved the same success as Mr. Gann did with Proposition 4.

Chapter 2

1980–1989: Transition and Uncertainty

California public libraries today are still an important community cultural and educational presence, a $200 million operation. The problem remains how to provide the excellent library service California citizens expect, given the limited amount of society's resources currently available to libraries.
– Mr. Colin Clark, California State Library ("California Pegs Proposition 13 Impact," Library Journal, 1980a)

There were no tax-related measures on the November 1980 California ballot. This did not mean that Californians were happy with the current tax structure. A 1980 Fall survey revealed that 78% of respondents felt state and local taxes were somewhat or much too high (Mathews, 1981). In 1977, the year before Proposition 13, that number was 70% (Mathews, 1981). The dissatisfaction had grown, as did a layer of speculation to the concern regarding Proposition 13, that is, as the 1980s unfolded, would California libraries be forced to continue decreasing services due to untold budgets cuts to come?

In the 1978 CLA report, *Special Survey of California Public Libraries*, Proposition 13 was held responsible for "a twenty-two percent reduction in library service hours, twenty-one percent cut in staffing, a decline of twelve percent in circulation, a decline of eight percent for reference services, and a twenty percent cut in funds for materials." The use of volunteers rose 282%.[1] In fact, Mr. Colin Clark noted, some library outlets were only staffed by volunteers as the paid staffed members were laid off.

In 1980, the CSL released *Survey of California Public Libraries 1978–1980 Before and After Proposition 13* seemed to highlight a reversal of the damages. It stated that libraries "regained the dollar position libraries held two years ago." However, CSL's Mr. Clark pointed to one fact that indicated not all was well, "During the two-year period we have suffered a twenty-five percent erosion in buying power … through inflation. The one percent increase in expenditures expected

---

[1] The Los Angeles Public Library System saw a jump from 7,200 volunteer hours to 44,000 hours between 1978 and 1982.

Proposition 13 – America's Second Great Tax Revolt:
A Forty Year Struggle for Library Survival, 39–57
Copyright © 2019 by Emerald Publishing Limited
All rights of reproduction in any form reserved
doi:10.1108/978-1-78769-017-220181002

in 1980 over the 1978 funding level is actually a twenty-four percent decrease in purchasing power."

The February 1980 issue of *Library Journal* (1980a) reported that operating revenue was still 2% below 1978's level. This led to fewer library buildings, fewer hours, fewer programs, fewer staff, and an indication that libraries would be forced to continue decreasing services at least in the early 1980s.

The funding concerns did not end with the state and local governments. Rather, it extended to the federal government. California Libraries received 8% of their income from the federal government, coming mostly from the staff program CETA and revenue sharing. As noted by Mr. Clark, "The continuation of this (federal) funding is also very uncertain .... And libraries have been living off their own reserves and carryover funds and this cannot continue indefinitely."

Mr. Clark explained the effects Proposition 13 had exacted by 1980:

- An 18% drop in staff positions (2,511 less people employed).
- A 22% drop in outlets (branches, stations, mobile library stops) from 3,857 to 3,027.
- A 23% decline in the hours of service. (Most affected are morning, evening, and weekend hours.) (*Library Journal*, 1980a)

The reduction in personnel lead to long queues for material checkout, piles of unshelved books, and backlogs in many areas, including overdue fines, reserves, and processing.

Acquisition budgets had made back all but eight-tenths of 1% of the initial 17% losses. Book budgets totaled $27,689,816 in 1978, $22,827,713 in 1979, and $27,456,911 in 1980. However, as mentioned earlier, inflation diminished the real purchasing power of budgets whether restored or not. Mr. Clark feared that "the acquisitions lost to libraries will in some measure never be recovered." He believed that large-scale retrospective purchases to be "unlikely and missing titles will soon go out print" (*Library Journal*, 1980a).

The *Survey of California Public Libraries 1978–1980 Before and After Proposition 13* provided additional statistics. Although close to $42 million was distributed in state bailout aid in 1979 and 1980 and federal aid grew each year from 1978 to 1980 (for each year respectfully: $13,480,873, $14,737,030 and $16,047,618). Local library funding still dropped by 18% overall. Particularly harsh was a 32% drop in county funding and a 45% drop in aid to special districts. For city libraries' operating income dropped by 1%, and for county libraries, operating income dropped by 3%.

In regards to dollars spent on personnel, there was a mix of good and bad news. Initially, personnel budgets went down; however, they did rise up to exceed the 1978 level: $126,942,377 (1978) $116,074,715 (1979), and $127,109,307 (1980) (*Library Journal*, 1980a).

The Berkeley Public Library attempted to recoup lost funding through public support at the polls. A tax measure, Proposition E, was proposed that, if passed, would give the library a $2.4 million budget. That dollar amount is nearly equal to what the library had before Proposition 13. The tax measure would ensure the library budget for the next 10 years with an indexing of the budget to inflation at a rate of 7%. Library supporters built a public relations campaign using the slogans "Libraries are your best bargain" and "Keep libraries alive." It was believed that the cost of funding Berkeley Public Library would be $45 per household. Proposition E was the first of its kind and it passed. Berkley Public Library director Ms. Regina Minudri stated voting against the library would have been akin to voting against "mothers and apple pie." This allowed hiring to begin, increased the hours of operation, and provided more money for the book budget ("Berkeley Calif. Library Takes $$ fight to the Polls," *Library Journal*, 1980b).

The Public Library Report for 1980[2] highlighted how Proposition 13 undercut community service programs provided by public libraries and cutback the hours of service, materials bought, and library staff. Eighty libraries responded to the survey: 83.8% indicated a cutback in programs, 65% blamed the cutbacks on Proposition 13, 27.5% experienced staff cuts, 18.8% reported cuts to the materials budget, 15% responded that they had cuts in hours or outlets were closed, and 7.5% reported bookmobiles have been idled. A positive note, 16.3% reported an uptick in their programming due to a new building, special funding, or the hiring of staff members with particular talents. Half of the libraries had to cut services geared toward children in such areas as story hours, film programs, and class visits. Worse, a few branch locations had to end all children's services.

Adult programming also felt the imposition of limitations by Proposition 13. Thirty percent of respondents had cut films, arts, and lectures geared toward the adult population. Outreach programs to shut-ins and hospitals were cancelled by 12.5% of respondents. Another 12.5% had to eliminate or rein in their display and publicity activities. Fifteen percent of libraries were able to enlist volunteers or friends to manage programs formally run by paid staff. As an aside, the Stockton Public Library noted Proposition 13 reinvigorated the Friends of Stockton Public Library after a dormancy of seven years. They hoped to help the library by raising funds.

Commenting on the *Public Library Report for 1980* was California State librarian Mr. Gary Strong, "With less publicity, fewer displays, reduced materials, staff, and hours, a library becomes increasingly less visible in the community, less able to serve those needing information and recreation. With fewer programs and less outreach activities, a diminished number of citizens may become involved with the library and be made aware of how it can enrich their lives. There will be fewer voices speaking up for the library at budget hearings, and this can only contribute to the downward financial spiral we are enduring in public library service in the 1980s" ("Calif. Community Programming Hurt by Proposition 13," *Library Journal*, 1981a).

---

[2]No attribution to *the Public Library Report for 1980* could be found. The fact that Mr. Strong commented on it lends credence to the report's findings.

User fees in California for public services went up, by some accounts dramatically, to include the use of leisure activities such as tennis courts and libraries as well as fees for education, electric power, paramedics, parks, roads, and sewers. In a survey conducted in 1982 of 19 cities with populations greater than 100,000, approximately 75% of fees were higher in comparison to pre-1978 levels. Cities with populations of less than 100,000 raised nearly two-thirds of their fees; lastly, counties raised the majority of their fees as well as initiating hundreds of new charges. This was a practice that reached into the 1990s.

In 1980, Mr. Howard Jarvis happily reported that California's economy had outperformed the nation's economy since the passage of Proposition 13. This was underscored by the US Commerce Department attributing 2% of California's rise in personal income to the proposition's passage. Property taxes did decline, although property tax revenues increased by approximately 13% annually because of rising property values and the rapid turnover of real estate that established a new tax rate based on the sale price. Mr. Jarvis pointed to the 7,500 homeowners who were defaulting on their property taxes each month prior to the passage of Proposition 13 and stated: "Now no elderly citizen or minority can say he or she can't afford to own land" (Scherer, 1980; Willis, 1981).

> *Well, I'll give him another twenty minutes, but that's it!*
> *– Mr. Howard Jarvis from the movie* Airplane!

Simply put, Mr. Jarvis was the more gregarious between he and Mr. Gann. This enabled a bit of celebrity status to accompany him. A few years earlier, commenting on his newfound celebrity and possible endorsements, he stated: "Don't look for me to jump into bed with just anybody. I'm too old for that" (Brodie, 1978).

There were ways that he found the passage of Proposition 13 financially rewarding beyond the savings he received being a property owner. The William Morris agency contracted Mr. Jarvis for television talk shows: $1,500 college campus lectures, and $5,000 business meetings. It was William Morris that suggested he write his book and there was talk of a movie about the tax fight. The movie did not come to fruition.

In 1978, he was a guest on *The Tonight Show* starring Johnny Carson and in December of the same year he met British Prime Minister Margaret Thatcher.[3] In 1980, Mr. Jarvis appeared in film and went on a book tour. His film credit was a cameo in the movie *Airplane!*,[4] playing a taxi cab passenger who waits patiently throughout the entire movie for the return of his cab driver. The driver does not return, yet the meter keeps running. The quote above is the last sentence of the film, coming after the credits, explaining how he will give the driver just one last chance.

---

[3]Prior to Proposition 13, he had met British Prime Minister Winston Churchill at the White House during United States of America President Dwight D. Eisenhower's administration.

[4]In Australia, Japan, New Zealand, Philippines, and South Africa it was titled *Flying High!*

His book tour was to promote *I'm Mad as Hell*, a book he co-authored in 1979 with ghostwriter Mr. Robert Pack. Within its pages he advocated for a smaller government (including a limited number of government employees), discussed the elimination of property taxes and his belief that sales tax (with some exemptions) and "other forms of taxes" are fairer than property taxes, "I would like to see property taxes cut out entirely, not just in California, but in every state that now has such a tax ... Income taxes are fairer than property taxes because they are related to ability to pay."

Turning to Mr. Paul Gann, his partner in getting Proposition 13 on the ballot, he contends that Mr. Gann wanted the two of them to become, "highly paid officials in the tax movement." Of which Mr. Jarvis said he would not do, that he "was not going to be paid anything for my work on taxation." He also believed, Mr. Gann was "jealous" of all the publicity he received.

For his part, Mr. Gann called Mr. Jarvis "irrational" that he has "a very difficult problem with the English language. It's hard for him to get above a two-letter word" (Scherer, 1980). He went on to say that until Proposition 13, Mr. Jarvis had been "an utter failure" (Jarvis & Pack, 1979).

The year 1980 saw Mr. Jarvis continue to push the tax revolution with the initiation of another proposition, Proposition 9. Placed on the June primary ballot it took aim at state personal income taxes with the goal of cutting them by 50% and eliminating every money bill currently before the California State legislature (Berry, 1980). Mr. Jarvis declared it a crime that the state would collect taxes while sitting on a $3 billion surplus and that California "hasn't done a damn thing" (Willis, 1981) to cut spending because of the surplus. In arguing for Proposition 9 Mr. Jarvis once again took a swipe at libraries, "If the kids can't read, what is the use of library books?" ("Revolt R.I.P.? This time Jarvis fails," *Time*, 1980).

That stance surely did not allay the fears of the many within the library community who believed that the passage of Proposition 9 would eliminate the money that was used to bail out libraries after Proposition 13.

Allies Against the Tax Revolution

In an attempt to defeat Proposition 9 the CLA worked collaboratively with publishers to create an awareness campaign called Know 9. On a nationwide basis publishers estimated that 85%[5] (Hearne, 1985) of their juvenile book sales were to libraries, giving them a particular interest in defeating tax limiting initiatives.

McGraw-Hill provided 5,000 posters with the slogan, "Libraries are good for business." The campaign ran radio and television public service announcements and initiated statewide distribution of fact sheets and publicity kits.

Berkley Public Library director Ms. Regina Minudri explained that prior to this campaign effort libraries were often "the best kept secret in town" and that

---

[5]By 1985, some publishers were claiming that figure was approximately 25% (Hearne, 1985).

they were going to "keep the library in front of the public" by doing a better job of publicizing their services. Based on lessons learned in the fight against Proposition 13, Ms. Minudri informed that they will not be "overstating the potential damage to libraries" by "sticking to the facts." An example of such a fact was that library services cost about three cents a day (Berry, 1980).

Citizens for Tax Justice, a combination of labor unions and public interest groups, joined the Know 9 campaign. This organization originated the year before, 1979, to counter the anti-tax movement created by Proposition 13. The organization is still in existence today as a Washington DC-based think tank.

The May 1980 editorial of the *Library Journal* (1980b) expressed the view that it was vital to recognize the attacks (Proposition 9 and Proposition 13) in California as a national problem and not the issue of one state. The editorial quoted economist Mr. John Kenneth Galbraith who suggested the attacks were "a struggle against those who see government services, including libraries, as somehow inferior to private goods and services." Mr. Galbraith stated that it was up to those of us who believed in the validity of public services – public libraries – to begin to assert, in every way we can, that "public services are not, in any respect, inferior to private goods and services. Public libraries are not less virtuous than private libraries..."

The *Library Journal* (1980b) concluded its editorial by asking those who believed that Proposition 9 was as dangerous for the rest of the country as it was to California to donate money to Citizens for California. This group was to mount opposition to the expected media campaign in favor of Proposition 9.[6]

Mr. Jarvis' encore was not the success that Mr. Gann experienced. Proposition 9 was defeated, receiving only 39% of the vote on the June 3, 1980 primary ballot (*Time*, 1980) The CLA, the *Library Journal*, Citizen's for California, Citizens for Tax Justices, civil service unions, other civic organizations, and publishers were successful in convincing voters that it would benefit the rich and cut government services to the poor. Further, Californians did not feel there was certainty with regards the impact that both Proposition 13 and 9 would have and thus were reticent to enact the fiscal limitations that Proposition 9 contained. Governor Jerry Brown, noting Californians had seen a $26 billion tax reduction over three years, did not see this defeat as the end of the tax revolution but rather as "a pause" (*Time*, 1980).

The groups that banded together for the defeat of Proposition 9 had practiced organized resistance. Those behind the Know 9 campaign had a predecessor experienced in organized resistance who was to join them.

In the summer of 1978, 17 days after the passage of Proposition 13, the Coalition to Restore Quality Library Services (the Coalition) was created. It was the brainchild of two temporarily laid off Alameda County (City of Freemont) library workers.

---

[6]Underscoring the thinking that what happens in California might spread eastward, a 1983 US Advisory Commission on Intergovernmental Relations reported that since Proposition 13 state spending has increased at a slower rate with the exception of states that are oil-reliant.

A few days after Proposition 13 became law, they had gathered 100 people to discuss organizing in support of the library. Membership evolved – reported as high as 245 people – to include interested citizens, nonprofessionals, management, and professionals from both the Alameda County Library and other Bay Area libraries. The Coalition began their awareness campaign by selling t-shirts. The profit made from the sale of t-shirts was used to broaden their message via fliers, press releases, mailings, and phone calls.

Their intent was to save Alameda County libraries and support state funding of library services. In fact, the Coalition was given credit by Alameda County Library Budget Analyst Mr. Dennis Miga for helping to get the library opened as quickly as it was. He singled out the public pressure they put on supervisors as making a difference. Similarly, State Senator Mr. Jim Nielsen who authored the aforementioned Senate bill (SB) 958 credited them for SB 958's passage out of the Senate.

It is interesting to note that most of the laid off Alameda County library workers were back at work within three months. That did not begin a precipitous end to the Coalition as news reports had them advocating for libraries until 1982. Since 1982, no mention of the Coalition was found.

Their unorthodox approach was not immediately welcomed by some within the library community specifically the American Library Association (ALA), the CLA, and the CSL. Support did come from some of the members of these institutions. This support combined with their process of specific strategies for each targeted entity: local governments, the state legislature (where they kept a continuous presence) professional organizations, community organizations, and the media enabled them to win over those who were at first indignant. The Coalition became known as reliable, credible, and a good source of information with a solid reputation backed by the public's support.

In fact, the CLA began providing complimentary exhibit booths at conventions and involved the Coalition in CLA lobbying activities in Sacramento and in the campaign against Proposition 9. CLA executive director Mr. Stefan Moses wrote to ALA executive director Mr. Robert Wedgeworth extolling the Coalition's virtues: "I think the Coalition is one of the few truly innovative and vital responses that we have seen coming from the recent attacks on library funding" (Parikh, 1980).

Partnering with the Women Library Workers, other Bay Area library organizations, and the Berkley Public Library led to a newsletter detailing the Coalition's efforts, welcoming people to get involved, and brought light to the financial struggles libraries were enduring.

Another aspect of the Coalition strategy was reaching out to librarians. They advertised their t-shirts in professional magazines, published articles, and developed a nationwide circulation of 1,500 for their newsletter. The Coalition communicated with librarians by participating in conferences, symposiums, and workshops. They reached aspiring librarians by speaking to library students at the University of California-Berkley and San Jose State.

Many of these endeavors took place out of California specifically in New York and Massachusetts. In time, they began to receive daily letters from librarians interested in their efforts as well as seeking help in using t-shirts to raise awareness. Librarians suggested the Coalition bring the t-shirts to bake sales, fairs, and radio station events.

Additionally, they were in constant contact with associations, community groups, guilds, and unions. Some linked to libraries and some not. The goal was to communicate beyond the sphere of libraries so that others within the community were aware of the issues faced by libraries. The hoped for result was greater community support for libraries.

Lastly, the use of media played an important part in helping the Coalition to manage the message. They learned who the reporters were to increase their chances of coverage and ensure the accuracy of reporting.

> *Neither the promise of a taxpayers' heaven nor the predictions of shuttered schools and bankrupt city halls has come true. – (Willis, 1981)*

If the promise of a taxpayer's heaven did not materialize, tax savings indeed did. From 1978 to 1980, Californians had saved a total of $20 billion in taxes (Willis, 1981), yet the state government continued to grow, while their multi-billion-dollar budget surplus winnowed away leaving local agencies to begin feeling slightly tighter budgets as 1981 began.

Budget tightening should not be interpreted as budget reductions. Rather, local government budgets were growing, some years larger than they had before Proposition 13. In the 1970s, local government budgets had grown at an annual pace of 10.5%. In the first year of Proposition 13 (1978), their budgets went up an average of 1.1%, the second year (1979) they were up by 13.3%, the third year (1980) saw an increase of 11.7%, and the expectation for the fourth year (1981) was an average local government budgetary increase of 5.6%. The depletion of the state's budget surplus would limit the state's increase in expenditures to approximately 1.7% in the next fiscal year (1981–1982) budget. The cut in aid to local governments was estimated to be 1.4% year over year (Willis, 1981).

This effectively put the local government budgets on a rollercoaster. Sometimes the budget would go above the 1970s annual growth rate of 10.5%, sometimes it would go below it. Often times it left cities and towns looking for new sources of revenue and/or increasing old sources of revenue. It appeared that help would not to be coming from the federal government as the state was to lose $2 billion in federal funds through the proposed Reagan Administration tax cuts.

Cities were of the belief that voters would have to decide their priorities. Did they favor fewer public services or would they be willing to pay more in local taxes to keep public services?

The Californian citizen did not seem to view the issue in the same manner as politicians had presented it. In other words, to the citizen it was not a choice to cut public services or raise local taxes. It was akin to a line item discussion allowing some services to be cut while others maintained their funding.

Many local governments continued to be criticized as inefficient and wasteful of the taxpayer's money. Yet, with less revenue coming in, local governments leaned on those taxpayers despite their criticisms, as well as corporations, for additional funding. These new or increased sources of revenue came in many forms: increased business license taxes, doubling bus fares, citizen donations made to their local government, deferring maintenance, and charging for entry to the zoo are some examples of how local government filled the budget gap.

The city of San Diego faced a deficit approaching $8.5 million for fiscal year 1981–1982 (Mathews, 1981) and moved to cut library and park services while simultaneously planning the elimination of street cleaning and tree trimming. With public backing, to include rallies, one library closure in San Diego did not occur.

The County of Los Angeles Public Library published charts and diagrams to provide a snapshot of what had changed for them between 1977–1978 and in 1981.

Some main points:

- *An increased reliance on volunteers*: In 1978, volunteers worked for 7,487 hours for the year. By 1981, that number was greater than 30,000 hours.
- *Decreased circulation*: In 1978, yearly circulation totaled 12 million items; by 1981, the number was 9.5 million.
- *Received less funding via property tax revenue*: In 1977, 82% of fiscal year funding was property tax revenue; by 1981 that number was 33% ("Los Angeles Co Shows How to Communicate Fiscal Gloom," 1981b).

In September 1982, the *Library Journal* reported the ominous news that the state legislature is considering the elimination of $5 million in funding provided to library systems and the State Library under the California Library Services Act. Calling it "another nail in our collective coffin" ("Threat to California Library Aid," *Library Journal*, 1982). California State Librarian Mr. Gary Strong explained that the loss of this funding would cause the State Library to lose one-third of its operating budget, and the flow of state dollars to cooperative library systems would stop.

Mr. George Deukmejian Jr became governor of California on January 3, 1983.[7] As a member of the California State Senate he had opposed Proposition 13. For governor he campaigned as someone who would not raise taxes and would balance the budget.

Governor Deukmejian cut $1.1 billion from the budget as he attempted to correct a $1.5 billion budget deficit. He believed the state had absorbed too much of the burden created by the loss of tax revenue and sought to restore the pre-1978 financial relationship between the state and local government. In this manner, he intended to end the bailout funding and submitted a budget that contained cuts to local governments totaling $108 million.

His budget proposal lacked the mandatory library aid per SB 358. The CLA and library supporters had lobbied for SB 358. It authorized, for the first time, direct library aid of $23 million for basic public library services.

---

[7]In 1982, Governor Jerry Brown did not run for the third term choosing to run for the United Stated Senate and losing to San Diego Mayor (and later California Governor) Mr. Pete Wilson.

Governor Deukmejian reasoned that given the fiscal crisis "we have generally not incorporated unfunded costs of legislation enacted separate from the budget" and asked the legislature to "consider these measures in view of their costs and the 1982–1983 budgets' projected deficit" ("California hedges on SB 358 funding," 1983).

Despite a clause to provide a 3% cost of living adjustment totaling $165,000, the 1983–1984 budget allocated less money for libraries than had been in the previous fiscal year budget by a total of $387,000 ($19,021,000–18,634,000).

Governor Deukmejian reversed course for fiscal year 1984–1985, adding $4,315,000 to the CSL budget. That figure combined both state operations and local assistance programs. Acknowledging the "early signs of program success" ("California State Library Budget Boosted by Over $10 Million," *Library Journal*, 1984a), Governor Deukmejian added $212,000 to the state library's administration of the California Literacy Campaign. He did indicate that funding beyond 1984–1985 will depend on a program effectiveness review. Funding was doubled for the Public Library Foundation from $6 million to $12 million. Interlibrary loan net lenders funding increased by $1,300,000. Net lenders were responsible for submitting claims under the Transaction-based Reimbursement Program[8] (reimbursing a portion of the cost to local libraries that extended lending services beyond their normal clientele). Design plans for a new CLA building were advanced by an additional $525,000. (Both the Public Library Foundation and the Transaction-based Reimbursement Program no longer received money after the fiscal year 2010–2011 budget.)

The additional funding was welcomed news. The heretofore lack of funding had continued to put a strain on library services. This strain did not go unnoticed by the public. A study released in 1985 showed the public's belief that libraries (along with education, street maintenance, and recreation facilities) were "the most salient areas of decay" since the passage of Proposition 13 (Gorman, 1995).

One way that libraries could better position themselves for increased funding and then begin to reverse the decay is by showing value to the community. Even in the most unique ways. In 1980, energy prices in California doubled. People would visit the Palm Spring Public Library to avoid the use of their own air conditioner. At this time a survey administered by the mayor's office showed that less than 1% of respondents would be in favor of cutting the library's budget. That was a more favorable response than the one received by the police department and its budget.

The 1980s continued the trend that began in the 1970s with citizens in other states trying to replicate California's tax initiative. In 1984, the Oklahoma Tax Limitation Committee introduced State Question 577.[9] This was a petition for a statewide election (vote) in an attempt to reduce their property tax ceiling. It

---

[8]From the California Library Services Act. Used for within state interlibrary loans and to enable out of county residents to check out books.
[9]State Questions are Oklahoma's initiative process.

would result in a reduction of more than one-third of the collected property taxes. Libraries and their supporters were opposed to the measure believing that individuals would realize only a small tax savings and public libraries would be attempting to function under a severe budgetary loss. In the end, State Question 577 was abandoned ("Oklahoma Tax Revolt Drive Menaces Public Libraries," *Library Journal*, 1984b).

> 'Since Prop 13 passed, bureaucrats and politicians have searched for ways to subvert the will of the people of California. – Mr. Howard Jarvis speaking to the need for Proposition 36 (Gunnison, 1984)

The ambiguous nature of Proposition 13 often placed it at the center of litigation. By the Summer of 1985 there were 81 court cases, 56 new statutes and resolutions, 32 attorney generals' or legislative counsels' opinions, and eight amendments at statewide elections designed to define and implement Proposition 13 (Throckmorton, 1997).

Many proponents of Proposition 13 felt the court had created loopholes within the law. Mr. Howard Jarvis and Mr. Paul Gann reunited and were joined by economist Mr. Arthur Laffer in an effort to get Proposition 36 on the ballot. The petition for the initiative was successful, gathering between 1,012,450 and 1,263,698 signatures, putting Proposition 36 onto the November 6, 1984 ballot. The intent of Proposition 36 was to close their perception of court-created loopholes within Proposition 13. Serving as the main authors, Mr. Jarvis and Mr. Gann argued that the courts had allowed local governments to collect taxes in the form of fees and assessments, circumventing Proposition 13's stipulation that a local government cannot increase an existing tax or impose a new tax without the approval of two-thirds of the qualified electors. According to Mr. Jarvis, "This will stop the phony practice, for example, of changing a garbage tax into a sanitation service charge to get around Proposition 13" (Gunnison, 1984).

They reasoned that the courts had ruled new taxes to not be increases, thus not subject to voter approval, allowed loopholes that excluded citizens from voting on new taxes, allowed the renaming of taxes as fees or assessments to avoid voter approval and had allowed assessors to "unfairly overcharge taxpayers hundreds of millions of dollars more than provided for under Proposition 13" ("Taxation California Proposition 36," UC Hastings Scholarship Repository, 1984).

Their argument came with a warning; if left unchecked, the anti-13 forces would next be targeting the 1% property tax limitation contained within Proposition 13. In fact, they claimed that this has been proposed on two other occasions and they feared a failure to pass Proposition 36 would mean the billions in tax savings related to Proposition 13 will be lost amid the increases in taxes and fees.

The opponents to Proposition 36 made it a point that they did not oppose Proposition 13. Proposition 36 opponents included the California Chamber of Commerce, the California Tax Payers Association, the State Superintendent of Public Instruction, the California Parent–Teacher Association, the Los Angeles County Board of Supervisors, and the American Association of Retired People.

They wrote a rebuttal to Mr. Jarvis and Mr. Gann and separate from the rebuttal an argument against Proposition 36. They viewed Proposition 36 as "long, complicated, and counter-productive" that it was "a tax shift not tax reform" and was not "in the spirit of Proposition 13." They accused Mr. Jarvis and Mr. Gann of creating a "slick, well financed public relations gimmick" employing "scare tactics" in seeking public support for a proposition that was no more than a "redistribution scheme." Mr. John Hay president of the California Chamber of Commerce referencing Proposition 36 called it "horribly flawed and poorly written and researched" ("Progeny of Proposition 13," *Time*, 1984; UC Hastings Scholarship Repository, 1984).

The parties who formulated the above rebuttal and argument were joined by the library community in opposition to Proposition 36. The CLA feared that the total effect of reduced budgets would be even greater than the 5–40% cut in support that was predicted. Their rational was based on the fact that lowered local government support would make libraries ineligible to receive new state aid under the Public Library Fund. It was reported in October 1984 that libraries had begun to list possible areas to cutback such as book buying, staffing, capital improvements, and branch closings. Los Angeles County librarian Ms. Linda Crismond believed that 23% of the staff would be cut and 15 library closures would occur if the proposition were passed. Moody's and Standard and Poor's advised that they would consider dropping California's bond rating if the proposition was passed.

The proposition did not pass. Proposition 36 was defeated by 851,379 votes: 4,904,372–4,052,993 (54.8%–45.2%) (UC Hastings Scholarship Repository, 1984).

Yet another measure to strengthen Proposition 13 was initiated and made its way to the 1986 ballot. Proposition 62 Voter Approval of Taxes was initiated by the California Tax Reduction Movement, an organization created by Mr. Howard Jarvis and his wife Ms. Estelle Jarvis to safeguard Proposition 13 and fight higher taxes. (The organization was later renamed as the Howard Jarvis Taxpayers Association.) Mr. Jarvis summarizing the pro-proposition point of view stated, "In 1978, Proposition 13 returned the power to control tax increases to the people, where it belongs. However, the State Supreme Court twisted the language of Proposition 13 in a 1982 decision which took away your right to vote on city and county tax increases."

Those who agreed with Mr. Jarvis believed the proposition would bring back "rights the State Supreme Court took away from us, [that] we [Californians] won with Proposition 13" (Throckmorton, 1997). It passed on November 4, 1986. Unfortunately, Mr. Jarvis did not witness the vote as he had passed on August 12, 1986, at the age of 83, from complications of a blood disease that had begun in 1982.

The proposed state budget for the fiscal year 1987–1988 was met with a mixed bag of good and bad news by the library community. On the plus side would be the continuance of or increase in funding for the automation of the state library's card catalog and information systems, funding for online reference systems, increased shelving capacity, and purchases of rare western history and genealogy materials. The unfortunate news was the proposed 1% across the board budget cut, leaving the State Library with a net increase year over year of $66,000. Despite requests for increases, it was proposed that there would be no increase in funding for local assistance programs administered by the CLA; the Public Library Foundation will stay at $20 million, and the California Library Services Act would remain the same at $11.6 million ("Governor's 1987–88 budget released in California," 1987a).

As it came to be the request for increased funding was heard as the legislature and Governor Deukmejian agreed to: increasing the California Literacy Campaign by 12.4%; bringing the California Library Services Act to $12,108,000; $200,000 in additional funding was allocated for the Public Library Fund bringing its total to $20,200,000 ("Calif. State Library Gets Increases for Literacy & More," *Library Journal,* 1987b). The automation of the card catalog and information systems, online reference systems, increased shelving capacity, and purchases of rare western history and genealogy materials were approved as proposed. Further, there was funding for the cost increase in materials.

One area of disagreement between Governor Deukmejian and the state legislature was over a $659,000 legislative augmentation to fund the working drawings for the State Library Annex Building. The governor vetoed the augmentation. That was not the last word on the subject; the Department of General Services requested funds in its 1988–1989 budget to complete the working drawings. All told, the State's Library budget for fiscal year 1987–1988 was $56,465,000 (*Library Journal,* 1987).

The sidebar goal to Proposition 13 was to reign in a growing bureaucracy. That goal may have occurred at the local level, where local governments and school boards lost 50% of their property tax revenue after Proposition 13 was passed; however, it came at the expense of a growing state government. Even though Proposition 13 was successful in providing billions of dollars in property tax relief, one 1988 estimate was $15 billion per annum (Will, 1988), and in moving California from fourth (1977) in state taxes to 24 (1988), it did not cut state spending the 15% that was anticipated (Weir, 1988). The less than expected cut in state spending combined with greater control of allocating collected property taxes effectively strengthened state government while weakening local governments and school boards. This weakened position made them ever more reliant on the state for funding while the citizens were less able to control how their tax money was spent.

This was the case as now local governments and jurisdictions were going to Sacramento for money, rather than the taxpayer for the approval to raise revenue. The state saw the opportunity to provide money to local governments while simultaneously taking away control and undermining autonomy. Although complementing Proposition 13 for being "a lifesaver for the people" (Weir, 1988), this power shift unsettled Mr. Gann: "That's one reason why 13 will one day be rewritten. Local governments lost, but the state government did not lose a penny. I did not intend that and neither did Mr. Jarvis" (Weir, 1988). Insisting that "we have to fix it" (Weir, 1988), Mr. Gann alluded to a proposition that served as a 13+; it would "cut the state's tax base and add that money to the local governments' tax base" (Weir, 1988). Underscoring the power shift was the 1988 joint legislative budget committee report that termed Proposition 13 as "probably the single most significant change made in the way governments, at all levels, operate in California" (Mathews, 1988).

School Library Insufficiencies

In 1987, a California Department of Education study detailed that the collections (available resources for student use) within school libraries had become insufficient, so much so as to have fallen below the level required to meet basic school needs.

By 1988, the lack of money within the California school systems had begun to press on maintenance, construction, and the school libraries. Many school libraries had to close or cut back on hours of operation, the total cost of deferred maintenance was nearing $150 million and more than $11 billion (McNulty, 1988) was needed for new school construction. To hedge against this and spurred by restrictions in the government's ability to raise and spend revenue – be it Proposition 13 or the other limitations imposed since Proposition 13 – in 1988, an education coalition led by the California Teachers Association was able to pass Proposition 98 to guarantee a minimum funding for the public school system.

> *The certainty of what each individual ought to pay is, in taxation, a matter of so great importance that a very considerable degree of inequality ... is not near so great an evil as a very small degree of uncertainty. (Adam Smith, Author, Economist, Philosopher)*

Proposition 13 fostered other changes beyond that of the relationship between the state government and the local governments. It also created a shift in the tax burden, as more of the onus had fallen from older homeowners to younger homeowners. (A similar scenario developed within the business community.) This shift, along with impact fees, had created a situation where new homebuyers were subsidizing public services.

To wit, the property tax of a home purchased pre-1978 was based on the assessed full cash value as indicated on their 1975–1976 tax bill. Conversely, if a home was purchased in 1978 or after the assessment was based on current market value, this structure provided certainty; however, there was a complicating factor. Between 1978 and 1988, the median price of a home had doubled in California, creating the dynamic of similar houses with greatly different property tax bills.

Mr. Paul Gann took note of the tax shift burden and was hopeful to enact a change: "My only regret is there isn't some way, and I keep looking for a way, that we can adjust this thing so my neighbor doesn't pay more property tax on the same valued piece of property than I pay" ("Some Key Players Reflect on the Impact of Proposition 13," *Los Angeles Times*, 1988).

Ms. Anna Shores, an assistant librarian, owned an Orange County home with her husband, Arthur, since 1957; both voted for Proposition 13. She believes it is not fair that they are paying a smaller property tax bill than their neighbors with similar homes. Ten years after casting their ballots, she explains their vote as a result of taxes "going up and up and up until our taxes were higher than our house payments. But of course it affected the schools. We didn't realize the full impact of it then. We voted for it strictly for survival" (Woo, 1988). The upside is that they pay only $265.60 per annum in property taxes. A downside is that they once shopped for a new home on the beach and decided staying put was their best option because of the $3,000–4,000 property tax bill that would rest on top of a larger mortgage.

With less revenue being generated from residential property, construction of new commercial property became more appealing to local governments. The building of a shopping mall generated a 6% sales tax, of which California cities kept 1%. Cities also collected revenue from hotels by means of transient occupancy taxes that ranged from 6–10%. Additionally, commercial property construction does not require the increased public services that often accompany new home construction. Therefore, the commercial taxes collected do not have to be earmarked for libraries, police, childcare, or other public services the general population relies on. It is important to note that the manufacturing industry was not seen favorably either, as manufacturing plants do not pay local sales tax.

Tipping Toward Libraries

The Fall elections of 1988 netted many positive outcomes for the library community, including a 64% success rate on library-related referendums.

Libraries and library supporters worked for three years with the legislature to put Proposition 85, the *Library Construction and Renovation Bond Act of 1988*, on the ballot. The $75 million proposition passed 52.7%–47.3%. Unique in its way as it was the first time the state of California had issued a bond to fund libraries. Twenty-four library projects could trace their funding back to Proposition 85. The CLA played a key role in these construction projects (Hall, 1990; T.G., 1988).

An even greater percentage of voters came out to support an even bigger bond for libraries in San Francisco where 76.2% of voters approved a $109.5 million bond to fund the construction of a new central library. The director of the San Francisco Public Library Mr. Ken Dowlin spoke after the vote, "Although our citizens are interested in the past, they don't want to live in it." The San Francisco Public Library was ready for the moment as they began the process of getting the new central library built within a week's time of the bond's approval (T.G., 1988).

In Santa Monica, 70% of voters approved Proposition JJ. This $4.5 million bond was issued to purchase and improve land adjacent to the main branch of the Santa Monica Public Library.

Berkley Public Library director Ms. Regina Minudri, who earlier in the decade participated in defeating Proposition 9, was once again actively campaigning for the sake of her library. This time she went door to door to get out the vote in favor of doubling a library tax. The doubling of this tax would increase the library's budget to $6 million per annum. Her hard work paid off as the tax was approved 67.8%–32.2%. Ms. Minudri stated, "We did our best to get out the vote" (T.G., 1988).

In rural Modoc County 67.99% voted for a levy increase equal to $18 per person to provide operating funds for the library (T.G., 1988).

Not all locales enjoyed election night 1988.

> *Every great city is measured by the quality of its libraries.*
> *– Los Angeles Mayor, Mr. Tom Bradley (Harris, 1988)*

Los Angeles' central library, along with three other facilities, were closed and many libraries within the Los Angeles Public Library system had been damaged by either arson or the 1987 earthquake. Further, 13 branches did not meet earthquake safety codes, eight of these branches were near closure due to this failure. There were branches waiting for expansion, remodeling, or were placed in rented storefronts considered less than acceptable. Meanwhile, three vacant lots stood idling as the lack of funding turned the promise of "a new branch library will be built on this site" into empty words.

Proposition L (for library) had the support of city and state politicians, including Los Angeles Mayor Mr. Thomas J. Bradley. Basketball icon Mr. Pat Riley, labor unions, the president of the school board, and chambers of commerce, all voiced support for Proposition L. Mr. Ray Bradbury, Mr. Charleston Heston, and Mr. Irving Wallace co-chaired the "Yes to Proposition L" campaign. Mayor Thomas J. Bradley and Ray Bradbury praised librarians as well as libraries when speaking of Proposition L.

There was monetary support, speeches given on its behalf, a letter campaign, ads went up, people were walking the streets to spread the word, political arms were twisted, editorials were written in its favor, and the library community participated every step of the way. A consulting firm, Cerrell Associates Inc., was hired to direct the message that Proposition L would allocate $90 million for 30 library building projects. Central to those projects were earthquake reinforcement and expansion of 15 branches, the building of four new branches, and the reopening of two branches that were closed because of earthquakes.

The strategy almost worked; 62.38% of the votes cast favored the proposition – 514,588 votes for, 310,385 votes against. The bond was a local initiative. As stipulated in Proposition 13, a two-thirds majority was required for a local initiative to be approved (Reagan, 1990; T.G., 1988).

The failure may have been traceable to the opposition of Councilman Mr. Nate Holden, who had issues with one method of funding for the Central Library project and campaigned against Proposition L. That method included tax breaks to private investors via a sale–leaseback arrangement of the Central Library. Mr. Holden quoted a cost of $10,000 in ad buys to help defeat the measure. After the proposition was defeated, Mr. Holden commented, "I feel great about it. I view this victory as a defeat against City Hall. . . It's almost like when I ran against City Hall and the people elected me. They said they wanted me to be their watchdog, and that's what I'm doing" (Harris, 1988).

Knowing that a two-thirds majority was within reach library commissioners looked toward the April 1989 election as an opportunity for a second chance.

Proposition L was renamed and reworked into Proposition #1 the Branch Libraries Facilities Bond. True to its new name, it did not contain a provision for the Central Library project.[10] The outreach for Proposition L was restarted for Proposition #1, complete with mailings, speeches, and gaining grassroots support. Proposition #1 passed with 68.2% in favor. The Los Angeles Public Library system would receive a $53.4 million upgrade (Reagan, 1990).

In addition to the changes mentioned above there were other factors that lead to Proposition #1 garnering the two-thirds vote needed that Proposition L could not obtain. Proposition #1 did not have the opposition that Proposition L had. Learning from Proposition L, Proposition #1 had a specific campaign for the San Fernando Valley[11] based on the construction of three new branches, while the rest of Los Angeles received a message focused on the earthquake codes. Lastly, there was a redesign of the distributed literature that was described as "brightened" with "more punch" (Reagan, 1990).

Shasta Public Libraries received the bad news in the Fall of 1988. But the story started in June when the northern California county library closed. The voters did not approve library funding in a special election that was held in September 1988 and in the November election library funding was not considered at all as it did not appear on the ballot. There seemed to be the notion, amongst voters, that the county had the money and was using the library to make a point. The county did in fact find money to reopen the main library and one branch on a streamlined no book-buying basis. The reopenings was facilitated by money the community was able to contribute (Berry, 1989; T.G., 1988).

Across the nation, 1989 was a successful year for the library community. Seventy-five percent of the library-related referendums were passed.[12] The total amount approved was $266 million out of a possible $395 million or 67.34% of the amount put to a vote with bonds being the most popular form of referenda (Hall, 1990).

California cities were collecting 17% less tax revenue per person in 1989 as compared to 1978, the year Proposition 13 was passed, increasing the importance of libraries in California to do well at the polls. They did fare well; Californian voters passed four measures that totaled $166,560,000, or 62.62% of the funds put to a vote were approved (De Courcy Hinds, 1991; Hall, 1990).

The frequency of library measures increased in the post-Proposition 13 California world. In the 10-year period of the 1980s, there were 36 such measures, in the 20-year period of 1990–2009 there were 272 measures. The average approval rate for all 30 years, 1990–2009, was 53.7% (Hall, 2010).

What are the key roles in the effort to gain approval of a referendum that is beneficial to the library community? According to library directors the significant issue of a successful referendum is the library building, be it improvements to an

---

[10]Money was obtained for the Central Library project separate from Proposition #1.
[11]San Fernando Valley was considered a key council district that Proposition L lost and would be needed for a Proposition #1 win.
[12]Library referendums had a 78% success rate for the years 1987–1989 (Hall, 1990).

existing library building or construction of a new library building. Library directors also mentioned quality of service offered by the library, the public relations effort in support of a referendum, proper organization of the campaign effort, support from the Friends programs and/or the Library Board, and the timing of the vote.

On the other hand, library directors believed that the raising of taxes was the most significant reason for failure of referendum. Other factor is the timing of the vote. Particularly Spring votes, as they had a relatively low success rate of 64.06% compared to the other seasons combined 89.33% success rate. Also hindering the passage of a referendum were the economy, and a highly organized opposition (Hall, 2010).

Library directors also spoke of campaign methods, believing that the use of pamphlets, factsheets, and bookmarks were the most effective campaign methods. Considered the least effective were hiring a public relations firm or consultant, television spots, and pre-vote polling.

> *They should be tried for murder, because if you give it to some-one, it's a death sentence.*
> *– Mr. Paul Gann commenting on those who knowingly trans-mit Acquired Immunodeficiency Syndrome (AIDS) (McQuiston, 1989)*

The end of the decade met with the death of Mr. Paul Gann. He passed away on September 11, 1989, at the age of 77. Mr. Gann died of pneumonia complicated by AIDS. He left us while being a patient at the Kaiser Permanente Medical Center where he was admitted after breaking his hip due to a fall at home nine days earlier. Mr. Gann had contracted AIDS via a 40-pint blood transfusion during a five-way open-heart surgery in 1982 when there was no means to screen blood for AIDS.

California took note:

- Governor George Deukmejian recognized Mr. Gann as "a tireless crusader on behalf of lower taxes, fiscal responsibility, and good government." He and Mr. Howard Jarvis "will be remembered for leading the modern-day version of the Boston Tea Party."
- To honor his memory the state Senate adjourned for the remainder of the day.[13]

Holding no remorse toward the one who donated blood for the transfusion, "the person could have been perfectly innocent." He believed his war on AIDS to be his "gravest responsibility ... more so than anything I've ever done, actually" (McQuiston, 1989).

---

[13]The Assembly had left before the announcement of his death.

He cosponsored the AIDS initiative Proposition 102 with State Representative Mr. William Dannemeyer. It was highlighted by the requirement that doctors report to state health officials the names and addresses of those who carry AIDS and anyone they reasonably believe to be infected. It was defeated with 34.41% "yea" votes to 69.59% voting "nay," or 3,208,517 to 6,116,276 votes respectively.

He did fight for the criminal prosecution of those who knowingly spread AIDS as well as advocating for more AIDS testing and mandatory reporting of the names of those who had contracted the virus.

In 1990, the Paul Gann Blood Safety Act became law in California. It mandated doctors to have a discussion with their patients regarding the risks of blood transfusions.

It was 1987, when Mr. Gann made public that he had AIDS. He commented that fighting AIDS may be "the last campaign of my life" (King, 1987).

Chapter 3

1990–1999: In Like a Lion Out Like a Lamb

> *Our life is March weather, savage and serene in one hour.*
> *– Ralph Waldo Emerson,* Representative Men: Seven Lectures

Like early March weather in the northern United States, the 1980s for library funding was stormy, unsettling, and unpredictable. However, due to victories at the polls it ended as calm as a late March day mimicking spring. Was this the beginning of a trend toward library funding stabilization or a temporary lull in the continued winnowing of budgets?

By July 1990, the United States was in a mild recession that would last until March 1991. This alone can be a disruptive force for a library's finances. In this instance, the recession was a bitter ingredient to be mixed with the tax revolt, giving the two the combined force to interfere with many aspects of library life in the early 1990s.

Reports in January 1991 set the state's budget deficit at $6 million, leading to California's local library funding budget losing $4 million (Quinn & Rogers, 1991). Reports in January 1992 detailed a $7,990,789.00 cut from the California State Library budget. A 13.4% drop from the preceding years' $59,842,000 (Quinn & Rogers, 1992).

In 1991, the State Library singled out Butte, El Dorado, Fresno, Shasta, Tehama, and Placer as the counties suffering the greatest financial hardship.

In an effort to cope with smaller budgets, both the University of California-Berkeley and the University of California-Riverside reduced serials spending. University of California-Riverside library director Mr. James C. Thompson laid the blame for their financial woes on Proposition 13, the recession, and a population boom that put an emphasis on increased services for the states' citizens.

However, it wasn't simply places but people the tax revolt and recession disrupted. Some sought early retirement. Others, as librarian Ms. Ginnie Cooper could attest, moved to new locales. Yet she faced old problems. Ms. Cooper was director of California's Alameda County Public Library from 1981 to 1990. Prior to her appointment as director, Alameda County Public Library was forced to

Proposition 13 – America's Second Great Tax Revolt:
A Forty Year Struggle for Library Survival, 59–79
Copyright © 2019 by Emerald Publishing Limited
All rights of reproduction in any form reserved
doi:10.1108/978-1-78769-017-220181003

shut down due to Proposition 13 funding cutbacks. Her charge was to bring the library system back into operation with redesigned services. By working with state and local officials as well as the local community she was able to obtain the financing for new library buildings and operations.

In 1990, Ms. Cooper accepted the directorship of the Multnomah County Library in Oregon. In doing so, she also stepped into the challenge of the city of Portland's spin-off of Proposition 13. The Oregon Property Tax for Schools and State Operations Amendment or Measure 5 was enacted in the same year she became director.[1] It bore similarities to Proposition 13 in many ways. Measure 5 was highly contentious, and was recognized as the beginning of the Oregon tax revolt. It capped property taxes at 1.5% over a five-year period. Like Proposition 13 the debate over Measure 5 was replete with the opposition warning of chaos if it passed and proponents believing an adjustment to government spending was in order. It too transferred more authority from local government to the state government ("Oregon Ballot Measure Five 1990," Wikipedia, 2018c; "Oregon Property Tax for Schools and State Operations Measure 5 1990," Ballotpedia, 1990).

Ms. Cooper faced a $3 million budget cut that would result in the layoff of approximately 50 people, reduce the library's hours of operation for all branches, and reduce the ability to purchase materials. Acknowledging the library's situation, and making a commitment to change it, the county did restore $2 million to the budget. This helped to minimize the number of layoffs, although less branch hours and a reduced book budget were still in the offing (Good, Better, and Best Are Relative Terms in Portland, 1991).

Ms. Cooper did not indict Measure 5 and the recession as the only causes for the budget tightening. She also pointed to the fact that two-thirds of the funding comes from a property tax levy that is only adjusted at three-year intervals. In an effort to raise money Ms. Cooper initiated eight successful campaigns to increase library funding for projects such as the construction of new buildings, remodeling and renovating older buildings, and expanding services. Ms. Cooper helped establish the library foundation and then worked with them to bring approximately $15 million in gifts over 13 years and established fees for certain services. She remained in Multnomah until 2003 when she accepted the position of executive director with the Brooklyn (NY) Public Library and then to the District of Columbia Public Library as chief librarian, executive director in 2006, where she remained until 2013.

By the mid-1990s the public library state rankings for California were 47th in the nation in total library books, 47th in full-time librarians per capita, and 40th in collection expenditures (Welch, 1996).

The Public Policy Institute of California issued a report showing the combined reduction in spending received for libraries and parks. In 1978–1979, 10% of city expenditures went to libraries and parks. In 1995–1996, this number was 6%. Budgets had become restrictive to the point that multiple copy buying was

---

[1]Ms. Cooper also had two additional measures related to property tax assessment pass while she was director at Multnomah County Library: Measure 47 in 1996 and Measure 50 in 1997.

less of an occurrence and low circulation periodicals were more likely to be targets for cancellation.

Naturally, libraries continued to provide the best service that they could possibly do under these trying circumstances. As evinced, the Palm Springs Library signed a five-year agreement (1996–2001) with the city of Palm Springs that both enhanced services and provided the necessary funding for these services. The library's obligations were: a minimum of eight full time equivalent (FTE) librarians, a minimum spend of $210,000 on new acquisitions for year one of the agreement with $5,000 increases in the years to follow, 55 hours of operation over a six-day week, and the maintenance of automated circulation, the public access catalog, CD-ROM's, and the internet. The city funding was $1,583,326 in the first year, with an annual increase of 1% in each succeeding year. The library may raise money for additional services or capital purchases as they see fit (Kristl, 1996).

> *We used everything in our bag of tricks*
> *– Mr. John M. Adams, Orange County Public Library director*
> *regarding 1992 financial struggles. (Gaughan, 1992)*

Although studies found that Proposition 13's financial burden to nonessential services – defined as services other than public safety to include libraries, parks and recreation, and street maintenance – may have been negligible,[2] it was certain that the proposition had a continued financial burden on libraries.

After a six-month delay due to the city's budget deficit, the Sacramento Public Library did expand its central library and reopen in 1992 with a two-day ceremony that received nearly 18,000 patrons checking out 9,000 books. The $31.9 million cost masked funding issues ("Sacramento Central Library Opens Amid Budget Imbroglio," Aggarwal, 1992).

The Sacramento Public Library's budget was based on financing from both the county and the city. A combination of factors – Proposition 13, changing demographics, the exhaustion of bailout money, and the recession – had led to the state "having problems maintaining public services" as explained by Sacramento Public Library director Mr. Richard Killian. With less funds going from the state to the County of Sacramento, the county was unable to provide proper funding to the Sacramento Public Library system. Further, the funding situation was not limited to the central library. There was speculation that half of the county's 16 branches would have to close. This funding predicament was the reason that the new Central Library was short hours and short staffed (Aggarwal, 1992).

The six-story central library, viewed as an excess in design and accompanied by cost overruns, opened for 35 hours per week, the least amount of hours for

---

[2]A sampling of 101 California cities showed that expenditures for nonessential services dropped by a mere 3% of total expenditures from 68% to 65% between 1972 and 1997, yet rose during these years on a per $1,000 of state personal income from $137 in 1972 to $166 in 1997 (Hoene, 2002).

a metropolitan central library in the country. Through a City Council mandate all floors will be open though without personnel on the fourth floor (books) and limited personnel on the third floor (periodicals) (Aggarwal, 1992).

Mr. Killian acknowledged that, "the real challenge now is to find a way to get it (the central library) open for full service." He believes, "We've constructed a functional, attractive, and efficient new central library and we're proud of that" (Aggarwal, 1992).

Two years after the opening, the central library had managed to extend hours of operation by four to 39 hours per week; with some branches closed during the week, the central library still had an early closing time of 6 p.m.

Financial struggles in 1992 similar to that of the Sacramento Public Library could be found in many areas of the state.

- Alameda County Public Library reduced their materials budget.
- The County of Los Angeles Public Library was permanently closing ten branches, cut the book budget, periodicals budget, and reduced hours of operation.
- Ventura County Library considered ending bookmobile services, cutting the book budget, and cutting hours of operation.

On a positive note, the citizens of Berkeley voted in favor of extending Paul Gann's Proposition 4, The Gann Limit Initiative, with better than 87% approving (St. Lifer, & DiMattia, 1992).

And the Super Majority Should Rule

The framers never envisioned that a supermajority of 60 votes would be required to enact virtually any piece of legislation or to confirm nominees (Sen. Tom Harkin, 2013)

The November 1992 California ballot saw 88% of the parcel tax measures put before the voters not receiving the two-thirds vote. This circumstance resulted in missed opportunities to increase fire and police protection, add streetlights, and to save libraries from closing. Californians had spoken and the tax revolt was still on.

What became an open question was the efficacy of the two-thirds requirement to raise taxes found in Proposition 13. As it stood in 1992, Missouri was the only other state that had such a requirement. Some local politicians were discussing a change. A senior fellow at Clermont Graduate School of Politics and Policy Ms. Bebitch-Jeffe believed that when Proposition 13 was passed the details got lost in translation and what counted to voters was symbolism and sending a message. She believed that the failure of a Los Angeles police tax measure that received 59% voter approval was a hit at the gut of that symbolism. It was the third Los Angeles property tax measure to be defeated in 12 years, and as Ms. Jeffe observed, "The first nail in the coffin of Prop 13" ("Controversy over California's Proposition 13," National Public Radio (NPR), 1993).

What really appears to be happening is that Proposition 13 has finally taken effect. There was so much growth in the economy it was never felt, but the state has now acted to end the situation that's been in place for 15 years and is making localities assume the revenue reductions that Prop. 13 caused.
– Orange County Public Library director Mr. John Adams
(Kniffel, 1993)

For the fiscal year 1993–1994 budget the state shifted $2.6 billion in property tax from local governments to pay the states' obligation to public schools and comply with the lawful requirement of a balanced budget an action Governor Wilson, a Proposition 13 opponent, believed was merely the state reclaiming some of the bail out money it had given to local governments after the passage of Proposition 13.

Shifting money from California's local governments is equal to taking money from libraries. Statewide, this shift resulted in $47 million less going to public libraries, the closing of 25 libraries, and a 14% reduction in hours of operation (Marquand & St. Lifer, 1994; Turner, 1993).

The November 1993 elections eased many of the ups and downs that had become norm in library funding. Proposition 172, the Local Public Safety Protection and Improvement Act of 1993, was a half-cent sales tax hike that went into effect on January 1, 1994. It was expected to raise $714 million in fiscal year 1993–1994 and then $1.5 billion per annum. Although not specifically library-related, it was hoped that the easing of city and county budget concerns would in turn lead to increased library funding. Proposition 172 was the first California statewide sales tax hike to be approved via special election since 1979 and the only one within the 30-year period of 1980–2010 ("California Proposition 172, Sale Tax Increase," Ballotpedia, 1973).

On the local level San Benito County voted in favor, by 17 votes, for a half-cent sales tax that benefited both libraries and government agencies. Property tax hikes for the Santa Paula Union High School District Public Library and the Marin County Free Library easily won the required two-thirds voter approval (B.G., 1993).

Typically, not every funding increase was approved. Merced County Library fell 66 votes short of a half-cent tax hike. Mountain View Public Library was just shy of approving a bond that would have financed a new library building with 63.9% voting "yea" (B.G., 1993).

There were numerous ballot wins across the United States to increase funding for both academic and public libraries. The positive news stories emanated from Illinois, Michigan, New Mexico, North Carolina, Ohio, and Pennsylvania. The combined increases were $15.483 million in new taxes and bonds ("Most Libraries Fare Well on Nov.2 Ballot Measures," B.G. 1993).

The tax hikes granted in the 1993 elections both within California and across the country seemed to indicate an easing from the public's ideological position on taxes. One year after rejecting most tax measures perhaps Californians were thinking the tax revolt could be eased and did not need to remain the same.

What I tell you three times is true.
– Lewis Carroll, The Hunting of Snark

The notion put forth: Had Proposition 13 become an easy scapegoat for every ill that government was experiencing? As it seemed, those who opposed the proposition were of the mind that if they told the citizens that it was Proposition 13's fault, three times, it is true, and the citizens would believe.

By 1994, the state's budget surplus had become a $5 billion deficit. Believe it or not, the citizens were told; being short of funds or missing an opportunity to do well was the fault of Proposition 13. After all, Proposition 13 robbed the government of its property tax revenue. So the reasoning concluded, it is the proposition that led to less money for capital improvements, child protective services, education, fire protection, infrastructure, libraries, parks and recreation, police protection, probation, public health higher user fees, and more potholes.

From the outside looking in, New York City resident and California born Ms. Kathleen Lander explained that "higher local taxes are not a cure-all for urban problems," she noted, "I am paying real estate taxes that are 13 times higher" as well as "city income tax, high sales tax, fees, numerous surcharges, and taxes on telephone bills," yet New York City "is plagued with violent crime, reduced park and library services, unrepaired school buildings, and crumbling roads and bridges" (Adams, 1994).

Greater Success

No scapegoating was necessary in Alameda, Altadena, Oakland, San Francisco, San Jose, and South Pasadena as all received budget increases in 1994.

Voters in Alameda County restored the Alameda County Library's Albany branch to 33 hours per week with a 75% approval of a parcel tax (Degliantoni & St. Lifer, 1994).

Sitting seven miles apart northeast of Los Angeles lay Altadena and South Pasadena. They shared more than close proximity as both had libraries at the brink of reducing their hours of operation because of static budgets. Each organized grassroots efforts to advocate for increased funding (Degliantoni & St. Lifer, 1994).

The Altadena Library District received increased funding through Proposition A. A parcel tax approved by 85% of voters. It brought $430,000 per annum to the Altadena Library budget. The cost to residents was $29 per year, while commercial landowners paid within a range of $59–79 (Degliantoni & St. Lifer, 1994).

Altadena county librarian Ms. Mary Lou Wrigley expressed confidence that with the increased funding, the library's service "will only move forward" (Degliantoni & St. Lifer, 1994).

The South Pasadena Public Library received increased funding through Proposition L. A parcel tax approved by 69% of voters. It will bring $250,000 per annum to the South Pasadena Library budget. The cost to residents was in a range of $24–48, while commercial property owners paid $24 per quarter-acre (Degliantoni & St. Lifer, 1994).

The South Pasadena Taxpayers Association protested that commercial property owners had to pay more in taxes. They initiated a campaign using mailers and a spot that aired on public access cable accusing the library director of being overpaid. The Pro Proposition L grassroots organization responded to these claims with phone calls, letters, and precinct blocking.

In 1992, Measure N, a parcel tax initiative to provide funding to Oakland's libraries, was proposed and fell 700 votes shy, receiving 65.8% of the needed two-thirds majority to pass. It would have been in effect for a 15-year period, providing a total of $60 million (St. Lifer & DiMattia, 1992). Gone with the measure were the hopes of expanding both children's services and literacy programs, increasing hours, and restoring the materials budget. A change was coming as 19 months later Oakland voters passed a dedicated parcel tax, Measure O – Library Services Retention and Enhancement Act of 1994. It garnered 75% percent of the vote. It was the same as Measure N: $60 million in total over 15 years to the library's general fund budget. Single-family residential properties paid $29.28 annually, while multiple family dwelling properties paid $20 per unit annually. The main library was required to remain open for seven days per week and branches had a minimum requirement of five days to open per week. Many services will be revitalized: full children's services in every branch, afterschool programs, expanded literacy programs, enhanced business services, restoration of the materials budget, and the operation of an African-American museum and library program (Degliantoni & St. Lifer, 1994).

The funding efforts of the Friends of the San Francisco Public Library (SFPL) enabled Proposition E – Library Preservation Fund to obtain the necessary signatures to be on the ballot. It passed with 70% of the voters approving. The proposition provided the library with a budget for the next 15 years with a mandate to the city of how much additional money will be collected and earmarked for the library. It also required that there be a main library operated by the city and a minimum of 26 branch libraries with all 27 locations opened for at least 1,028 hours per week that being the fiscal year 1987–1988 service level. Additionally, it guaranteed funding for the library for the blind.

Proposition E garnered support from several newspapers as well as five members of the board of supervisors. However, it was opposed by Mayor Mr. Frank Jordan. He stated that he is in favor of libraries, that he liked the provision detailing the hours libraries should be open. Though he did not believe in budgeting by a charter mandate that came from the people nor the money attached to this mandate (Degliantoni & St. Lifer, 1994).

San Jose voters approved a benefit assessment district with the purpose of supplying $5.5 million per year for 10 years, beginning with 1995, for the San Jose Public Library system.[3] Sixty-five percent of the people voted in favor, leading city librarian Mr. Jim Fish to state that the vote was "a minor miracle for California." Single family residents were to pay approximately $25 per year while a proportional dollar figure will be instituted for apartment residents and businesses.

---

[3] The benefit assessment district was replaced in 2005 with a library parcel tax.

Mr. Fish commented that the library intended to use the money for the first "adequate book budget in anyone's memory." Other areas that were intended to receive additional funding included building maintenance, public services staffing, expansion of children's programs, and improving automation to enhance services and productivity (St. Lifer & Rogers, 1995a).

Less than Success

Despite the good news of 1994 by 1997 the SFPL was in financial trouble. The city board of supervisors took control of SFPL's finances and SFPL announced staff cuts that were largely directed toward temporary and part-time workers. The supervisors voted twice for supplemental appropriations totaling $4.1 million. However, SFPL was still $1.3 million short of its budget. Per a budget analyst report the financial dire straits that SFPL found itself in was attributable to disproportionate payroll expenses in an effort to meet increased use of the library. SFPL hoped to keep intact children's services, the circulation of materials, collection development, operating hours, and general reference. While adult programs, fee-based information service, online databases, and the telephone information program were all possible subjects to a service reduction (G.F., 1997).

For the second time in less than a year, the voters of Merced County rejected a half-cent sales tax that would have helped fund the Merced County Library. The June 1994 sales tax measure also fell short. Merced County libraries were unfunded by August 1994. In November 1994, the supervisors voted to close all 19 libraries. Through the use of volunteers, donations,[4] bake sales, and other fund-raising efforts, some libraries were able to remain open for three days a week. A December 6 vote by the board of supervisors did authorize the money to keep the main library open on a part-time basis (Degliantoni & St. Lifer, 1994; Jaffe, 1994; Schrag, 1994).

Los Angeles County, similar to Merced, suffered multiple failed ballot measures. This, combined with the existing lack of funding, lead Los Angeles County to close 10 public libraries (Jaffe, 1994).

Los Angeles County and Merced County notwithstanding 1994 was a pro-library year. California State librarian Mr. Gary Strong commented, "Success can be used in the future-success in public opinion breeds success. That gives me hope" (Degliantoni & St. Lifer, 1994).

> *We have to come to terms with a greatly reduced level of revenue.*
> *– Orange County librarian Mr. John Adams (Renee & Meyer, 1995)*

"You can pin this almost 100% on Proposition 13," said Mr. Dale Scott, a San Francisco financial adviser to local governments (Norris, 1994). He was referring to the events of December 6, 1994 when Orange County found bankruptcy to be

---

[4]Including some tip money from waitresses and public employee donations.

its only option.[5] This not only affected the county but also the 186 public agencies (such as cities, utilities, and schools) that had a financial interest in Orange County's investment pool. At that time it was the biggest municipal bankruptcy in US history. Since then Detroit, Michigan (2013) and Jefferson County, Alabama (2011) have exceeded Orange County ranking first and second respectively. Orange County's treasurer, Mr. Robert Citron, had invested the county's money in high-risk bonds and derivative securities. Mr. Scott referenced the fact that if not for the lack of funding created by Proposition 13, Mr. Citron would not have felt the need to generate revenue through high-risk investments. Mr. Scott stated, "The only reason people are out there trying to turn two dimes into a quarter is they can't finance basic needs anyway else. The Music Man comes in and says, 'I can get you 10 percent when everyone else gets 5 percent,' and he's a hero" (Norris, 1994).

Within a month of the bankruptcy filing Orange County supervisors were apprised of how tight the fiscal picture was; losses ranged from \$1.5 billion to \$2 billion. Amid the bankruptcy conversation was the contention that the upper class was not being affected by Proposition 13 and its aftermath (the bankruptcy) on the same scale as the rest of the population. This helped to establish the belief that locking in this type of disparity was a goal of Proposition 13's proponents.

The bankruptcy acted in the same manner for libraries as Proposition 13. That is to say, the Orange County Library System was expected to take a significant financial loss along with cultural, school programs, and recreation funding. Initial reports were that no branches had closed nor people laid off. However, downsizing was expected. As Mr. Adams noted there was an expectation of a \$5 million budget cut. He is hopeful that personnel will not be a part of the downsizing as previous hiring freezes and attrition had already reduced the workforce.

News then followed that all 28 branches had cut back to four days per week from six days with the possibility of further cuts as the library waited for the bankruptcy to sort itself out. Eventually six of the branches were schedule to close though personnel were expected to be spared. The plan was to sell the buildings that were closed and to extend hours at the remaining branches back to six days per week. The fallout continued to late 1995 as the city of Mission Viejo had seceded from the county's library system and the city of Irvine announced its intention to do the same ("City Secedes from Orange Co. Library," *American Libraries*, 1995a; "Another City Quits Orange Co. Library," *American Libraries*, 1995b; G.F., 1995; Renee & Meyer, 1995; St. Lifer & Rogers, 1995b).

School Libraries' Continued Struggle

Bankruptcy serves as a severe case of fiscal destitution. Yet, as illustrated, punitive budget cuts to library operations do occur within solvent municipalities. To wit, between 1982 and 1992, years before Orange County had become the first to file for bankruptcy, more than half of California's school libraries closed (Gorman, 1995).

---

[5]It is also believed by some that the 2012 bankruptcies of Mammoth Lakes and Stockton California can be traced back to Proposition 13.

By 1994, reports placed California as last in the ratio between librarians and students with one librarian for every 8,512 students contrasted against the national average of 1:820 (Reeves, 1994).

Only 32% of the school libraries had a certified librarian on staff. That number was 21% at the elementary level (Gorman, 1995). This left many students lacking the proper training to develop the library skills needed to become college ready or a lifelong learner. As Mr. Michael Gorman, dean of library services at California State University Fresno explained, it was just as common to have an 18-year old asking a basic computer question as it was an older returning student. Mr. Gorman expressed displeasure with cuts in education and suggested the need for "comprehensive … library instruction and literacy programs at all levels of education" (Gorman, 1995). He called for unity between academic, public, and school libraries across the United States as what happens to one type of library eventually affects the others both in-state and nationwide. He suggested enlisting library organizations, Friends programs, and educators to help restore library funding and services and that the library community should become more involved in literacy education.

The students who had access to library services did not necessarily have access to quality material. It was not uncommon to find books on the school shelf that were greater than 10 years old. In 1994, it was reported that some California school libraries had books predicting that man would land on the moon.

A contributing factor was that California dedicated only 78 cents per student for the school library book budget. This did not compare well with the national average of $7.47 per student (Gorman, 1995).

The mid-1990s struggles of California's school libraries were not seen by California's public libraries. Numerous measures put before the voters in 1996 were approved. The *Library Journal* (St. Lifer & Rogers, 1996) referred to this as the greatest success story of the election season.

- Alameda County voters passed a four-year utility users tax that will result in $1.25 million per annum for libraries. It passed with 67% of voters approving.
- In the city of Berkeley, voters passed $30 million in general obligation bonds. It passed with 67.1% of voters approving. The intent of the money was to expand, remodel, and seismic proof the main library.
- Voters in the city of Berkeley outdid themselves in a second measure with a voters' approval of approximately 90% for the continuation of a library operating tax.
- Voters in the city of Mill-Valley approved a Mello-Roos Community Facilities District tax to raise $4.6 million to expand and remodel their library.
- In the city of Oakland, voters approved a general obligation bond of $13 million for library construction projects.
- Sacramento's vote was a split decision. They were voting on a benefit assessment of $22 per residential parcel. With the need of two-thirds approval within the county, it received 58.3% votes. However, city voters passed the measure with a 62.7% approval while only requiring a simple majority. The city approval provided the library system with $3 million per year. The different voting standard was borne from county counsel calling the measure a special tax while city officials called it a property assessment.

- Santa Cruz's voters, both city and county, passed a 0.25 cent sales tax increase with a 72% approval. This added approximately $5.5 million per annum to the budget for the next 16 years.

As it goes in nearly every election there was a mix of results. Some of the losses for libraries included:

- The Coalinga-Huron Unified School District Library voted down, with 58% of the needed two-thirds approval, a $12 per residential unit parcel tax, which would have added $130,000 per annum in operating funds.
- In San Diego both the city and county voters did not approve a 0.25 cent sales tax increase missing the two-thirds threshold by 5.4%. It would have provided approximately $365 million over a five-year period.
- Orange County voters denied the Orange County Library District a parcel tax of $29 per unit. It was to be for five years and would have raised $460,000 per annum.

> ...the most revolutionary act in the history of California ....
> California State Association of Counties ("California Proposition
> 218," Wikipedia, 1996)

In 1996, the Howard Jarvis Taxpayers Association believed that there was a portion of Proposition 13 regarding special assessments that was not being enforced. Mr. Joel Fox, the association's president, stated: "A section of Prop 13 that said all local special taxes shall receive a two-thirds vote. Well, right away, people started saying, well, we can get around that term special taxes" (Jaffe, 1996).

Many felt the lack of enforcement stemmed from a vagueness and inconsistency in the wording of the proposition. This vagueness and inconsistency, they argued, required judicial interpretation to resolve.

The California courts found that mechanisms for raising local revenue were exempt from Proposition 13. The courts ruled that benefit assessments were not taxes under Proposition 13 thus subjected neither to the two-thirds supermajority nor the 1% limit of ad-valorem taxes.

Proponents of Proposition 218 claimed since the courts decisions were handed down special districts had increased assessments over 2,400%, cities increased benefit assessments 976% and utility taxes 415% (Cole, 1998; League of California Cities, 2017). Revenue from assessments did indeed go up, the State Assembly Revenue and Taxation Committee noted that four years after the passage of Proposition 13 assessment property tax revenue was $7.976 billion as compared to $5.561 billion in the fiscal year immediately following Proposition 13. This was in addition to increased fees, hidden taxes, and levies.

In search of rectification the Howard Jarvis Taxpayers Association sponsored Proposition 218 – Right to Vote on Taxes Act. In a simple and straightforward message they asked the citizenry to vote "yes" if they believed that they had the right to vote on taxes. As seen in their ballot statement they took advantage of distrust in politicians: "Under Proposition 218, officials must convince taxpayers that tax increases are justified. Politicians and special interest groups don't like this idea .... Proposition 218 allows you and your neighbors-not politicians-to decide how high your taxes will be" ("Voter approval for local government taxes. Limitations on fees, assessments, and charges," UC Hastings Scholarship Repository, 1996).

Those opposed were fearful that wealthy landowners, foreigners, and developers would have more voting power than the average homeowner. They anticipated cuts in public services in general, libraries specifically, and an overall destruction in the quality of life in California for decades. Its supporters believed that it would expand democracy and empower citizens.

On November 5, 1996, an 81-year separation between taxes and assessments was dissolved.[6] Proposition 218 was passed. The tax revolt continued, effectively narrowing local governments' ability to generate revenue through assessments, charges, and fees.

Colloquially it was referred to as Son of Proposition 13 or Prop 13: The Sequel. No matter the use of nickname Proposition 218 would become law effective July 1, 1997 putting local governments in the position of having to convince voters to raise taxes. As Ms. Stacey Simon[7] (1998a) wrote in *Ecology Law Quarterly*: "Government now has a product to sell ... government must now educate and inform the voters so that they may exercise their power to make fiscal decisions in a responsible manner." That is not to say the onus was all on the government as Ms. Simon pointed out: "The public, likewise, must learn about the issues it will be voting on, as people will ultimately have to live with the outcome of their vote." She pointed out, how crucial educating the public would be (through the government and the media) as many California residents likely did not know that they had the right to vote on all taxes. One official wondered whether the voters had bothered to read the proposition at all and concluded that, "they had no idea what they were voting on."

The legislative analyst's office provided an apt description: "As a practical matter, this requirement will mean that programs that benefit people, rather than specific properties – such as libraries, mosquito abatement, recreation programs, police protection, and some business improvement programs – must be financed by general or special taxes or by other non-assessment revenues" (O'Malley, 1996).

Mr. David Flint, the assistant director for finance and planning for the County of Los Angeles Public Library commented that across the state library officials began to sort out what Proposition 218 meant for their libraries. There was a December 1997 meeting planned at the California State Library in Sacramento to brainstorm solutions to the new amendment.

On the matter of procedural costs associated with Proposition 218, the Los Angeles County Library district was receiving $9 million dollars per annum from a new parcel fee that will not continue unless the library conducted a special election prior to July 1, 1997 at a cost of $1–2 million. Mr. Flint explained that if they

---

[6]In 1915, the California Supreme Court ruled that assessments were not taxes (Spring St. *v.* City of Los Angeles).

[7]A May 1999 J. D. candidate at the University of California at Berkeley.

did not continue to receive this revenue the library district will have to impose a 35% reduction in service hours and cut book budgets in 44 of the 89 branches ("Proposition 218 May Hit California Libraries Hard," Kristl, 1997).

Ventura County officials decided to not institute a library rescue plan with a special assessment district because of the $235,000 cost to hold the now required special election. County supervisor Mr. Frank Schillo confirmed the county would explore alternative financing options (Kristl, 1997).

The frustration due to procedural costs could be explained through the statement of an aide to the county supervisor of Santa Clara. Speaking with regard to the possible imposition of a $14 fee Ms. Andrea Flores remarked, "Think of all the tax dollars spent on this process, all to debate a ($14) fee. It makes no sense" (Patel, 2001).

Ms. Jackie Goldberg, Los Angeles City Councilwoman, commented on an ominous future for public services: "Probably a lot of streetlights won't be functioning. Probably the library hours at branches will be cut drastically. Probably the programs at parks and recreation centers will be cut drastically, as will upkeep of them. I think eventually what you'll see is that there won't be any city services left. You'll have police, you'll have fire. And you probably won't have much of anything else." Mr. David Flint had suggested that Proposition 218 "will probably be tied up in courts for some time" (Kristl, 1997).

These newly placed limitations on charges, fees, and special tax assessments gave impetus to the finding of alternative means to raise funds. In 1997, an initiative, to be known as SB 409, was created by the California Library Association (CLA) to transform the California Library Service Act (CLSA) into a multi-library funding act. Heretofore public libraries fared well under the CLSA but others, school, special, and academic libraries, did not. According to CLA president Mr. Gregg Atkins: "We're seeking about $15 million in transition funding for the next three to five years. CLA has laid the groundwork for this, and we are looking forward to a favorable hearing" (Watkins, 1997). It did pass and became law in 1998.

Proposition L and Good Fortune

> *I think it's something that surprised elected officials everywhere, because they never thought we could pull this off. –*
> *Ms. Sandra Reuben, Los Angeles County librarian regarding*
> *Proposition L (Flagg, 1997)*

In 1995, an assessment district was approved by the L.A. County supervisors to fund 41 of the County of Los Angeles Public Library's 87 libraries (Boehning, St. Lifer, & Rogers, 1995). However, neither state legislators nor fundraising campaigns by staff and library Friends were able to stop a shift of property tax revenue out of the libraries budget. The ensuing financial constraints forced 10 branches to close on Sundays; other branches reduced their hours of operation and purchased fewer books and computers. The assessment district was discontinued with the passage of Proposition 218.

On June 3, 1997, a special election was held in Los Angeles County. On the ballot was Proposition L, a special tax measure regarding libraries set to replace the funds lost through Proposition 218. This tax would raise $7.8 million per annum and would allow the library to maintain hours of operation, purchase materials, conduct programs, and avoid the elimination of approximately 300 combined full and part-time jobs. Proposition L exceeded the two-thirds majority passing by a near 70–30 margin. Ms. Sandra Reuben, the county librarian, stated that this demonstrated, "there's very strong support of public libraries here in California" (Flagg, 1997).

Ms. Reuben credited the library foundation and the library's union for their fundraising efforts as well as working the telephones in support of the campaign to pass Proposition L. Additional support came in the form of endorsements by every newspaper in the area and the neutral position of the Proposition 218 initiators, the Howard Jarvis Taxpayers Association. In total, the County of Los Angeles public libraries experienced a near doubling of their budgets because of Proposition L.

Los Angeles was not done receiving good news. The city library system, LAPL received an additional $1.2 million to the budget for fiscal year 1997–1998. The city council approved a 7% increase that will create 88.5 staff positions, keep the central library and eight regional branches open for seven days per week as well as keep seven community libraries open six days per week (Flagg, 1997).

Further, five new links of the central library with its branches in a resource-sharing virtual electronic library will be initiated. Said city librarian Ms. Susan Kent, "Los Angeles is a city that is committed to learning and to literacy. This commitment was strongly reinforced by the actions taken by the Los Angeles City Council and Mayor Richard Riordan. It is also tremendously appropriate that this has happened during our 125th anniversary year celebration" (Flagg, 1997).

The mayor allocated more funding than what the Los Angeles Public Library had requested and the city council increased the funding even further. The LAPL public information director Mr. Robert Reagan in an attempt to explain their good fortune pointed to 30 construction projects that were completed on time and under budget and stated that local government "have a tremendous respect for Susan Kent. We've shown over the years that the money they give us is well spent." Mr. Reagan also gave credit to the area's citizens, "these politicians get enormous feedback from the people who use the libraries" (Flagg, 1997).

> *In a society increasing fueled by information, libraries are vital not only to the intellectual but to the economic vitality of the state. – State librarian, Mr. Kevin Starr (Blumenstein, St. Lifer, & Rogers, 1998)*

The California State Library experienced a bottoming out of funding during the recession of the early 1990s. By the late 1990s, some characterized California's libraries as battered, dilapidated, and shrunken.

There was a turnaround.

The $86.9 million fiscal year 1998–1999 budget was the largest increase in the California State Library's 148-year history and a 27% increase over the previous year's budget (Blumenstein et al., 1998). Within the State Library's budget were funding increases for direct and inter-library loan programs, for the California Library Literacy Services program, the Public Library Foundation, and the acquisition of library materials. According to state librarian Mr. Ken Starr: "This governor (Pete Wilson) and this legislature recognize that public libraries are centers of information dispersal" (Blumenstein et al., 1998).

School libraries also received good news. They were budgeted for $158.8 million with the expectation that they will acquire computers and related technology (Blumenstein et al., 1998).

Directly following LAPL's $1.2 million increase came bigger news for fiscal year 1998–1999. Proposition DD was approved by 72% of the voters. The $178.3 million proposition will provide money for the renovation, expansion, and/or replacement of 28 branches. Libraries will be built in four neighborhoods heretofore without library services. The branch buildings being replaced were expected to be twice the size, earthquake safe, and disabled accessible. LAPL was looking forward to the upgraded branches having multiple services not necessarily available in older buildings, including computer-training centers, children's storytelling areas, and community meeting rooms. City librarian Ms. Susan Kent commenting on the vote stated that it was a reflection of "the very high regard that the people of Los Angeles have for their libraries and their equally high expectations of the library" (Berry, Blumenstein, Oder, & Rogers, 1998).

The good financial news for libraries spread to west to Santa Monica were 81% of the voters approved a $25 million bond and $1.5 million was allocated by the city council. The combined money was to be used to expand the main library and upgrade three branch libraries. In many cases local agencies were reluctant to engage in long-term planning because of the uncertain budget situations. That is not the case with Santa Monica. Expansion of the main library began 10 years earlier with the passage of a 1988 bond issue to purchase land next to the main library for expansion (Berry et al., 1998).

> *People always say you can't fight City Hall, but with Proposition 13, we did and we won. – Mr. Joel Fox, president, Howard Jarvis Taxpayers Association (Wildermuth, 1998b)*

Along with the arrival of 1998 came the 20th anniversary of Proposition 13. The anniversary brought back into focus the two-part story that swung between the need for property tax relief in 1978 and the overreach many thought Proposition 13 had turned out to be. Through those 20 years the law was seen nearly as profound as the New Deal with many politicians becoming less critical as it grew into the third rail of California politics. "People think it's the word of God, some kind of coming from the Almighty, and they shouldn't touch it," Mr. Ed Edelman, former Los Angeles County supervisor commented (Simon, 1998b). To wit, US House of Representative Ms. Jane Harman upon discussing a property tax system that would "lower someone's property taxes and share the lowering with the guy next door" insisted, "I am not going to touch Proposition 13" (Barabak, 1998). The Howard Jarvis Taxpayers Association believed: "No politician in his right mind takes on Prop 13 directly" (Cole, 1998).

Though many politicians were becoming reticent to criticize the proposition others were not. Writer Mr. Peter Schrag, regarding the once high national rankings of California public services that had dropped to near the bottom referred to proposition 13 as helping the "Mississippification" of California's public services.[8]

The tax revolt was still in existence despite the fact that by the early 1990s California was close to the national average in the amount of state and local taxes paid as a percentage of personal income. Looked at from a slightly different angle, the combined amount of state taxes, local taxes, assessments, and fees paid as a percentage of personal income ranked California 22nd in the country.

Californians were experiencing a booming economy in 1998, and the surrounding years, yet spending was below the national average for public library services, K-12 education, the arts, and transportation. San Mateo County's county manager Mr. John Maltbie speaking to the situation said, "Libraries, parks and recreation programs were all hammered. They've never been able to recover from Proposition 13" (Wildermuth, 1998).

National Public Radio (1998) labeled the highways and libraries as eroded. A patron noted the Richmond Public Library was once a jewel of the city describing its current state as "a little tarnished right now." Head librarian Mr. Joseph Green concurred, "It's going through some tough times" and then expounded, "You have to remember ... its going through the difficult times in the context that everybody is going through tough times" (Gonzales & Simon, 1998).

Proposition 13 continued shouldering the blame for near everything that went wrong from inefficient libraries, to potholes, to the cancellation of after-school sports, to an increase in retail development that led to suburban sprawl and dead-end minimum wage employment. Ms. Jean Ross, the executive director of the California Budget Project observed, "It has fundamentally weakened the whole public infrastructure of the state, from education to roads and everything in between" (Simon, 1998).

Conversely, the *Los Angeles Times* (1998) editorialized: "Proposition 13 is 20 years old and it's time to proclaim the tax cutting measure a success." The citizens agreed. A poll found that 60% of respondents felt property taxes were too high in 1977, while only 22% felt that way in 1998.

The proposition was also credited by State Assemblyman Bill Leonard and others as the seed from which the Reagan Revolution and the 1994 Republican Revolution grew. Mr. Steven Moore, writing for the Cato Institute (1998), credited Proposition 13 for being the beginning of the conservative movement.

---

[8]A 1998 *Los Angeles Times* poll of 1,409 Californians showed, 32% responded the proposition had a bad effect on public services and 29% respondent it had a good effect on public services.

By 1998, county supervisors held sway on only 3.3% of their general fund. Whither the other 96.7%? Mandated and controlled by Sacramento. Mr. Jarvis would often say, "It's them or us" (Simon, 1998). It became more them, less us after Proposition 13. Mr. Gann had recognized this power shift to the state and was of the mind to reverse it back to local government. However, the idea never gained the momentum necessary to make it a reality.

A myriad of actions were born from Proposition 13; library budgets fell and rose. Other propositions were initiated to close loopholes found in Proposition 13. A bifurcation occurred, easing the tax burden on long-time homeowners while increasing the tax burden on new homeowners. Billions of dollars were saved in property taxes although a large amount of that went to large property owners and corporations.[9] Assessments, exactions, fees, and charges for formally free services were raised by government[10] and subsequently limited by voter initiatives.[11] Local governments cut services. California went from a high-tax state to an average-tax state, and 1,100 of the 2,150 California library branches closed were attributable to Proposition 13 (Patel, 2001).

A Super-charged Democracy or a Threat to Democratic Viability?

California and Proposition 13 were given attribution for spurring the "initiative industrial complex." This occurred both within California[12] and across the country on issues beyond taxes and spending such as affirmative action, campaign reform, criminal law, repealing domestic partner laws, environmental protection, gambling, blocking a healthcare law, hunting, insurance rates, immigration, logging, marijuana legalization, regulating pigs and calves, eliminating parking violation fines, school policy, sugar production, term limits, and overturning a law granting illegal aliens the right to obtain California driver's licenses.

In the November 1996 elections, 90 initiatives were placed on ballots in 23 states. That was a high not seen in 80 years and nearly doubling the high of 41 in 1986 (Schrag, 1998; Walsh & Kulman, 1996). It also brought the fear of further restrictions on both local and state governments. Interestingly, a theory took hold that this was the beginning of the end of representative government to be

---

[9]The real dollar savings was indeterminate as governments increased assessments, levies, fees, and other taxes such as hotel, sales, and utilities, although it was estimated that commercial property owners received two-thirds of Proposition 13's tax breaks and immediately saved $4 billion (Wildermuth, 1998a).

[10]As a grouping, they were referred to as a Byzantine system of fees, assessments, and exactions.

[11]Per the California Taxpayers Association, the percentage of personal income that went to state taxes, local taxes, and fees was near identical in 1998 to 1977, i.e., 14% and 15%, respectively (Simon, 1998b). A field poll showed a near 2:1 belief that state and local taxes had increased enough to offset the tax reductions provide by Proposition 13 (Wildermuth, 1998b).

[12]California's qualified initiative totaled through the years: 1960s: 10; 1970s: 24; 1980s: 55; 1990s: 62; and 2000–2009: 60 (Secretary of State California, 2016).

taken over by instant communication initiative government. The result would see politicians being sent to "the scrap heap of history" (Schrag, 1998) and a general callousness that leaned against minority's rights and toward the potential of an unstable United States.

As it celebrated 20 years Mr. Peter Schrag commented that Proposition 13's legacy *is* government dysfunction and had created a lost sense of community. Mr. Schrag believed that every initiative reduced both the local and state government's ability to govern in a responsive, comprehensive way. It drove governments to further irrelevancy, ever more alienating the citizens, reinforcing the lessons taught by Proposition 13, and the world it had created. This in turn generated the pressure for even more initiatives. As a result, by 2003, more than half of the California state budget was based on constitutional formulas or other mandates.

Those who believed in initiative thought it still to be in the spirit of the grass-roots effort and populist sentiment that had originally spurred Governor Hiram Johnson to push for and pass into law the initiative process in 1911.

California citizens continued a lack of trust in and saw little accountability from their government. In particular, the local government. How come the library was closing? Why isn't the street cleaned? All too often, the response constituents heard was, "It's Sacramento's fault." The frustration derived from the situation led the citizens to want more control over governmental spending and decision making which was achieved through more initiatives. The use of initiatives was so great that it was sardonically suggested California enter a twelve step program to get over their initiative addiction.

A Different Proposition L: He Said, She Said

Proposition L, not the Los Angeles Proposition L from 1997 but a proposition with the same name from a different city in another year. This time the city was San Diego and the year was 1999. The proposition would add a quarter percent sales tax increase for five years, resulting in $423 million to fund all libraries within the county with a focus on holdings and technology ("San Diego Voters Trounce Library Sales Tax Measure", *American Libraries*, 1999).

The proposition was backed by nearly every elected official in San Diego County. It also had the backing of San Diego Mayor Ms. Susan Golding, the owners of baseball's San Diego Padres, the San Diego Union Tribune, the San Diego Taxpayers Association, the former city librarian, and a $650,000 campaign effort.

Opponents to the proposition were backed with less than $5,000 and included the former library commissioner, political figure Mr. Richard Rider, former San Diego Mayor Mr. Roger Hedgecock, and the grandson of Mr. Paul Gann, Mr. Richard Gann.

Mayor Golding believed, "It is extremely important that it pass, particularly now, because we have a chance in this city to have a first-class library system for everyone" (Rogers, 1999). The city council was also interested in upgrading the library system, as they had passed a financial plan for the construction of a new main library facility. When the voting was over, the only thing the two Proposition Ls shared was the name.

Barely 50% of the voters approved, short the needed two-thirds majority, marking it as a loss for libraries.[13] Mr. Richard Rider the chief opponent of Proposition L stressed, "Our explanation all along was that we're not opposed to libraries. We're opposed to the tax increase" (*American Libraries*, 1999).

Questions abound as to why it did not pass. Answers were as elusive as they were varied: Was it the out of town political consultant who proclaimed to be the winner of more California library bond issues than anyone else? Was it the strategy of holding a special election in the hope that low turnout would help libraries? Was it the too cutesy claim that the L stood for libraries? Was it the damage done to the city budget by propositions from the year before? Could it have been the scant possibility that a private management company might be interested in running the library system at a cost that could be millions less than the current budget? (Invariably, it would be brought up that privatizing public services would be beneficial, i.e., a private company could raise rates – in lieu of taxes – without having to go to the people for approval.) Or, could it have been the relative small amount of money spent to campaign for it compared to the amount of money spent by the hotel industry and sports interests for their government funding?

Library backers believed that it was bad timing and bad luck that defeated the proposition. Momentum was building in favor of the proposition passing as San Diego City Council member and chair of the regional library authority Ms. Judy McCarty pointed out, "The in thing to do was to support Proposition L." As the calendar moved to within several weeks of the election there was a shift in sentiment "from a vote to improve your neighborhood library to a vote will increase taxes" (*American Libraries*, 1999).

Backers believed that two events conspired to alter the citizen's sentiment. One was the anger that grew when the San Diego Padres dismantled their team by trading four star players five months after gaining voter approval to finance a multimillion dollar stadium expansion. The other was the continued skepticism of the government by the people. In this case the focal point of the skeptical view was on Mayor Susan Golding who was not able to convince the city council to secure $130 million from the expected $312 million national tobacco lawsuit settlement for a new main library. This caused the citizens to wonder why they should raise their taxes if the city was getting $312 million. Mr. Scott Maloni, spokesperson for "Yes on L" said, "I really believe the vast majority supported Proposition L but didn't trust local government" (*American Libraries*, 1999). Mr. Rider commented that people saw through the "misrepresentation" by politicians that there was no Plan B if Proposition L were to fail. He noted that those same politicians, within a day of the proposition not passing, suggested to the state legislature to reintroduce a previously vetoed bill (by Governor Pete Wilson) that would allocate to libraries the increased property taxes the county

---

[13]A similar measure was defeated three years earlier with a 58% voter approval.

was receiving from the housing boom. Unfortunately, diverting property taxes to libraries might not have helped in San Diego as Ms. McCarty pointed out, "property and sales taxes combined do not even pay for public safety" (*American Libraries*, 1999). Deepening the citizens' suspicion of politicians even more was the fact that there were Plan B's being proposed from mayoral hopeful Ms. Barbara Warden and Deputy Mayor Mr. Byron Wear.

Another interesting note occurred prior to voting: a lawsuit over the sample ballot. Superior Court Judge William Pate presided over a suit brought by Ms. Kathryn Sullivan, the president of Citizens Action for Local Libraries and a proponent of the proposition. She sought the removal of a paragraph contained within the sample ballot for Proposition L.

Opponents of Proposition L claimed that supporters of the proposition were making up facts. In the sample ballot, they alleged that supporters were making a claim that most San Diego libraries were falling short of the American Library Association's (ALA) minimum standards. Opponents continued that this was untrue since the ALA does not have minimum standards for libraries to meet. Ms. Sullivan wanted the paragraph containing this allegation removed, claiming that what the opponents were saying about the supporters was untrue. Judge Pate sided with Ms. Sullivan and ruled to have the paragraph removed from the sample ballot. Upon hearing this, one opponent of Proposition L, Mr. Edward Teyssier, commented, "The voters are going to get from the (sample) ballot that our libraries really don't comply with ALA guidelines, but there are no ALA guidelines. There are no standards." Mr. John Wertz the attorney representing Proposition L's backers, "The court has essentially noted that they (the opponents) lied (J. K., 1999).

A point of clarification: The ALA's Public Library Association in 1966 did publish *Minimum Standards for Public Libraries*. In 1980, the Public Library Association moved away from standards to a planning concept with the publication of *A Planning Process for Public Libraries*.

Libraries fared much better elsewhere in California:

- A $19.8 million bond, Measure E, was passed by voters in Fairfax and San Anselmo. It will upgrade computer labs, classrooms, and libraries within the Ross Valley School District.
- In Livermore 81% of the voters approved a $150 million bond measure. The money is expected to be used for a new community center, public school improvement, and a new library.
- Ross, San Mateo County, and Santa Rosa will fund both classroom and school library improvement via the passage of parcel tax measures.
- With 87% approval voters renewed a six-year parcel tax that generated $200,000 per annum or 20% of the South Pasadena Public Library's budget (*American Libraries*, 1999).

As Proposition 13's 20th anniversary became history and the decade closed out, it was clear that activism was a key component of the tax revolt.

Mr. Cyril Stevenson,[14] who had worked with Mr. Paul Gann and for the passage of Proposition 13 explained, "There was tremendous activism brought about by Proposition 13 and much of it still exists today." Perhaps, activism and Proposition 13 were best summed by President Emeritus of the Howard Jarvis Taxpayers Association Mr. Joel Fox, "Government is always looking for a loophole. If we didn't have taxpayer groups to constantly monitor what Sacramento is doing, we would have lost the protection of Proposition 13 long ago" (Wildermuth, 1998).

---

[14]Mr. Stevenson served as President of the California Republican Assembly.

Chapter 4

2000–2010: Good Times Bad Times in California and Countrywide

An amazing confluence of the library world, elected officials, and library advocates … we look forward to a golden age of library construction in California
– State librarian Mr. Kevin Starr regarding Proposition 14
(Rogers & Oder, 2000)

Bonds Library Bonds

Six times a fail, seventh time a charm. Library funding met with mostly positive results in 1999. This positivity carried over to 2000 as the California citizenry passed Proposition 14, the *California Reading and Literacy Improvement and Public Library Construction and Renovation Bond Act of 2000*. This was the state's first library bond since Proposition 85 passed 12 years ago. Proposition 14 was passed with 58.9% voting in favor. In terms of actual votes cast those in favor were 4,298,471, while those against were 2,994,289. This was the seventh attempt in the past 10 years to pass a state library bond ("California Proposition 14, Bonds for Libraries," Ballotpedia, 2000).

While not ceding financial decisions back to local government the $350 million bond will provide the opportunity for local governments to pick the projects they wish to fund from these four areas:

(1) Construction of new libraries.
(2) Expansion and renovation of existing libraries.
(3) Purchasing furniture and equipment.
(4) Upgrades to telecommunication and electrical systems to enhance technological services

Per the summary by California Attorney General Mr. Bill Lockyer Proposition 14 will also "expand access to reading and literacy programs in California's public education system" (Ballotpedia, 2000).

Proposition 13 – America's Second Great Tax Revolt:
A Forty Year Struggle for Library Survival, 81–94
Copyright © 2019 by Emerald Publishing Limited
All rights of reproduction in any form reserved
doi:10.1108/978-1-78769-017-220181004

The California State Library identified 425 proposals that were in need of funds. Many of these projects were delays resulting from the passage of Proposition 13. Although the California State Library noted that money would be distributed to as many libraries as possible, there was a process to be followed. A six-member board was responsible for the distribution of grants to local governments ranging from $50,000 to $20 million. Grant eligibility required a 35% match by the local government. Public and school libraries that entered into joint use projects[1] (AKA cooperative agreements) received first priority funding ("Calif. Approves 350 Million Dollar Bond," *American Libraries*, 2000; Rogers & Oder, 2000).

State librarian Mr. Kevin Starr was of the belief that Proposition 14 was the single largest bond issue of public money ever to be authorized for library construction in American history. He gave credit to the California Library Association for its efforts in getting the proposition passed.

Though some believed that the missions of public and school libraries were too different for joint use many still celebrated the proposition's passage. The interim director of the San Francisco Public Library (SFPL) Ms. Susan Hildreth believed it, "bodes well for library construction projects in San Francisco and throughout the state." Taking pride in the San Francisco electorate, she noted, "Proposition 14 was passed at the highest level in the city and county of San Francisco.[2] We are very happy about that (and) that SFPL Friends and foundation made the lead contribution to the statewide campaign." That contribution totaled $35,000 (Rogers & Oder, 2000).

Los Angeles' citizenry also voted yes in high numbers as 64.6% of the voters approved the proposition. According to Los Angeles Public Library director Ms. Susan Kent, "We worked hard to get the Los Angeles city council to endorse the proposition, which they did." Expressing the same exuberance as SFPL's Ms. Hildreth, she noted, "We're certainly looking forward to being able to apply for some of this money for enhancements to projects that we're doing. I think it is a real indication of support for libraries throughout California and a continued indication of support in Los Angeles for libraries" (Rogers & Oder, 2000).

The money from Proposition 14 was not generated as quickly as was the enthusiasm. Mr. Kevin Starr informed that regulations needed to be written, statewide public hearings regarding the regulations needed to be held, and then the state would have to approve those regulations. Once approved the treasurer would then offer the bonds for sale and the six-member board would meet to review applications. Naturally, time was required so that interested libraries can submit their applications. All told, Mr. Starr believed this to be a one-year process, at the least.

Once the regulations were codified librarians saw that the board had set a loose definition of joint use.

---

[1] As insisted by Governor Gray Davis before the bond act would be put before voters.
[2] The city and county of San Francisco voters passed Proposition 14 with a 77% voter approval.

Joint use meant the following:

- *Co-located*: A school and public library under one roof.
- *Joint venture*: The public library runs a student-orientated service. A typical example would be a homework center.

Additionally, there must be a signed cooperative agreement between the public library and the school district. This agreement must be in place for 20 years prompting library bond act manager Mr. Richard Hall to comment that the signed agreement is "going to make a difference ... so it's not just, 'Let's try to cooperate and if it doesn't work, let's forget it'" (Glick, 2001).

Either formally or informally most public libraries were already serving students. The stipulation of a formal agreement did not leave public librarians expecting significant changes to their job responsibilities. However, California Library Association president Ms. Anne Turner thought that getting a signed cooperative agreement would not be easy. She questioned what the expectations of school districts for public libraries were. Especially considering many of those school districts defunded their libraries in a Proposition 13 world. Mr. David Flint assistant director for finance and planning for the County of Los Angeles Public Library spoke directly to this issue, "We might say we'll provide space for a homework center, but we might negotiate an agreement where the district puts up staffing for the homework center – otherwise the school is getting a free ride and there's (nothing very) cooperative about it."

Mr. Hall felt that this approach could be advantageous. As he noted, it is not mandatory to have the school district contribute monetarily to a joint venture, but if they do, "money does speak loudly" (Glick, 2001).

> Embedded in the culture of the state.
> – Political analyst USC Ms. Sherry Bebitch Jeffe regarding Proposition 13 ("Recall election prompts review of California's sacred Prop. 13," Telegraph Herald, 2003)

The general sentiment, and what was evinced here, was that Proposition 13 foisted both intended and unintended consequences on state and local governments in the area of raising revenue and spending limitations. Ringing in 2003 did not bring in a change in sentiment. At 25 years old, there was no conclusion as to its efficacy. Proposition 13 remained simultaneously good, bad, and imperfect.

More exactly, Proposition 13 was seen as havoc ridden in its short term, served as a funding problem in the totality of its 25-year existence, believed to be undemocratic due to the two-thirds super majority, and moved politicians to phony hand-wringing over the possibility of lost services. It was perceived as an imperfect success hedging against unrestrained property assessments and demonstrating how the people can take a stand against government inefficiency and financial abuse.

The proposition continued to receive credit for saving California citizens and businesses billions in tax dollars. Further, it may have lessened an unfavorable impression of California as not friendly to business or the middle-class homeowner.

The power shift from local government toward state government, an unintended consequence described as seismic, was still present in the early years of the new century. This despite local governments' request for reform and state commissions, tasked with studying the issue, recommending reform. The failure of the state to act on this matter resulted in the continuation of the fiscal pressure local governments had felt since Proposition 13 was passed.

Californians still held a positive opinion toward the proposition. In the early 2000s one poll had the margin as narrowly favorable (May, 2003), while a *Los Angeles Times* poll found that voters would be inclined to vote "yea" at approximately the same percentage of votes garnered in 1978 (Hoene, 2002). This is an unsurprising development given that Californians overwhelmingly did not perceive Proposition 13 as a cause of a significant decline in services. According to Mr. Joel Fox, "Proposition 13 continues to give certainty to the taxpayer instead of the tax collector. The voters know that Proposition 13 is their taxpayer shield" (Carpay, 2003).

Some Libraries Included

Proposition 47, the Kindergarten-University Public Education Facilities Bond Act of 2002, was passed with 59.1% of the voters approving[3] ("California Proposition 47, Bonds for School Construction," Ballotpedia, 2002). Within the $13.05 billion bond was $384 million for library projects. Many of these projects benefited California State University (CSU) (Albanese, Oder, & Rogers, 2002; Ballotpedia, 2002). Ten years earlier, the dean of libraries at CSU Fresno, Mr. Michael Gorman had heard an administrator commenting that there would be no new libraries built because they would be empty. On the strength of the new projects in renovation, expansion, and construction, Mr. Gorman believed that Proposition 47 signified the central role of libraries at CSU.

Project highlights include the following:

- California State Polytechnic University Pomona, library renovation and expansion.
- CSU Fresno, library renovation and expansion.
- CSU Long Beach, library renovation and expansion.
- CSU Monterey Bay, new library construction.
- CSU San Marcos, new library information center.
- Community colleges will receive $77 million.
- San Francisco State University library renovation and expansion.
- San Jose's new university/city library equipment purchase (the San Jose Public Library and the San Jose State University partnered to create the Dr. Martin Luther King Jr. Library. Serving both the city and the university, the library opened to great success with a gate count of 11,998 on day one.)

---

[3]Note that Proposition 39, an amendment to Proposition 13, was passed in 2000, lowering the two-thirds supermajority to 55% for the passing of a school bond.

Additionally, Governor Gray Davis' office utilized lease revenue bonds to fund four CSU projects to include library construction at Monterey Bay and the San Francisco State University library renovation and expansion.

> *Librarians will be creative as they've always been. They'll look for funds and grants and pay for materials out of their own pockets. –* *California School Library Association Executive Director, Ms. Penny Kastanis (Ishizuka, 2004b)*

While university libraries seemed to fare well, school libraries began to take on water. When combined; counselors, nurses, and school librarians were among the worst ratio to students in the nation. By 2003, California had crept back into the mid-thirties (per state) in public school per pupil spending (Schrag, 2003). Yet no help to rectify the school library problem was coming from within the state budget. (In fact by late 2016 a California state audit ranked the state last in school librarian to student ratios.) With a projected state revenue shortfall of $12.5 million Governor Davis' proposed budget for fiscal year 2003 included a cut in school library funding from $100 million to $80 million (Sack, 2002).

After the gubernatorial recall in 2003, Governor Schwarzenegger wanted to condense the school library fund into a general education budget to streamline education spending. The library community held many concerns about this idea. It would not be good, they felt, for school libraries to lose a distinct budget line item. The library community also feared the possibility of schools diverting library money to other resources, the possibility of the end of the state-mandated plan of collaboration between librarians, teachers, and principals, and the elimination of guaranteed funding of all libraries in the states K-12 schools as provided by the Public School Library Act. They pushed back on Governor Schwarzenegger's idea via a rally and outreach to local legislatures, school principals, and school boards. The line item remained in the fiscal year 2003–2004 budget.

What did not remain was the support Los Angeles felt in 2000. Ten ballot measures designed to increase taxes for the funding of the County of Los Angeles Public Library system failed to pass in 2004 by not garnering the needed two-thirds supermajority (*American Libraries*, 2004). Of significance was the denial of a parcel tax increase of $25.26 throwing 10 cities into decision mode regarding a cut in library services. Los Angeles County Library spokesperson Ms. Nancy Mahr said, "Those cities won't have that cushion to fall back on." This also served as another setback to the Los Angeles County Library budget as Governor Schwarzenegger had already slashed $460 million in funding (Ishizuka, 2004a). triggering discussion of the closure of 16 libraries and the laying off 400 workers.

San Francisco also had a 2004 vote. They fared better. Voters passed Proposition H with a 70.77% voter approval, paving the way for a city fund for increased spending on education. A part of that money was earmarked for school libraries (Gewertz, 2004).

This small victory could not slow the pace of bad news when one considered the state's fiscal situation. The timeframe of January 1, 2003–June 30, 2004[4] engulfed the governor's office with a $34–40-billion budget shortfall. Governor Gray Davis responded with proposed $20.7 billion in cuts over a two-year period. Public libraries were a target within those cuts. They were to lose $28–30 million, seeing a reduction from $52 million to $22–$24 million or a 54–58% decrease. To help offset the cuts Governor Davis asked for legislation allowing libraries to charge user fees. These fees would help cover the administrative costs of direct borrowing and of interlibrary loan. Suggested fees were $1 for a book borrowed from a library outside the patron's county and $5 for interlibrary loans outside the patron's county. The library community was not pleased. Comments by Alameda County librarian Ms. Linda Wood summed up the sentiment, "The idea of these fees violates the fundamental philosophy of public libraries. I think the public would be outraged" (Eberhart, 2003; Flagg, 2003).

Many library systems had the good fortune of avoiding plans for branch closings with last minute dollars provided by municipal boards and councils. However, from Tehama County in the north through San Diego in the south, public libraries once again had to take action for the possibility of reduced funding. They leaned on Friends of the Library organizations as an alternative source of funding, cut hours of operation, closed branches for one extra day per week, increased overdue fines, and ended bookmobile services.

The Oakland Public Library received a cut of $875,000 (Flagg, 2003). It could have been worse. The original budget cut was to be $2.1 million. Still, the city of Oakland responded by eliminating 22 full-time equivalent (FTE) positions within the library system. That too was the lesser evil; the possibility of seven branch closures was floated when the budget cut of $2.1 million was proposed (Albanese, Oder, & Rogers, 2003). They did close from August 29, 2003 through September 2, 2003 (*American Libraries*, 2004). Further, the library planned to be closed for at least one day per month from October 2003 through June 2004 ("Shortfalls Prompt Shutdowns in Three Major Cities," *American Libraries*, 2003c). They also posted a book wish list on Amazon to compensate for a reduced book budget. An effective idea as it brought in over 600 volumes (Eberhart, 2003). Good news came via Measure Q,[5] increasing the library's annual parcel tax from $36 to $75 resulting in a $10.7 million boost to the Oakland Public Library's fiscal year 2004–2005 budget and approximately $9–10 million per annum until 2024. The measure enabled a course correction; the main library would be open for seven days per week, branches would be opened for six days per week, all branches provided children's services, and the materials budget was restored (Ishizuka, 2004b; "Oakland, Modesto Tax Measures Pass," *American Libraries*, 2004).

Ventura County lies 374 miles south of Oakland. In December 2002, Governor Davis wished a midyear cut to the public library fund. This came after an initial

---

[4]California Fiscal year ends on June 30.
[5]A reauthorization of the 1994 Library Services Act. Per library director Ms. Carmen Martinez, a failure to pass Measure Q would have netted a $1.1-million budget shortfall.

cut in September. The 70% proposed reduction was rejected by the legislature in January 2003. Had the public library fund been cut, Ventura would have received $201,500. At its highest point, the fund provided $750,000 to the Ventura County Library ("California Gov. Halves Statewide Library Funding," Flagg, 2003). The legislature's rejection allowed the Ventura County Library to avoid laying off 27 staffers and cutting the hours of operations at three locations.

The state's fiscal year 2003–2004 financial problems also put California State University and the University of California in line for budget losses. In anticipation of losing a combined $626 million the two university systems expected libraries, administration, fees, research, student services, and professional development to be affected (Albanese et al., 2003). To help facilitate a smaller budget CSU expected to reduce enrollment while the University of California, Los Angeles (UCLA) Library will cut academic journals and databases. Still, there was a real possibility that more cost-saving measures were to be needed immediately. "We have been warned that we may have to make additional midyear cuts," stated Ms. Barbara Schader, head of collection development, UCLA biomedical library (Albanese, 2003b). In fact, they did. Midyear cuts to the budget were indeed going to happen. The number under discussion went as high as $133.6 million in combined budgetary cuts (Albanese, 2003a). The two university library systems were considering leaving both full and part-time positions unfilled, delaying projects, and would spread the cuts between both administration and libraries.

In March 2003, Governor Davis had signed a budget cut of $11.6 million to school libraries (Flagg, 2003). Hit particularly hard was the San Jose Unified School District as they also lost a hoped for $6 million parcel tax that was seen as a means to maintain services. The deleterious effect of these two occurrences was the reassignment of 24 school media specialist to classroom teachers while two school media specialists were cut (Eberhart, 2003). It can be reasoned that some number of the reassigned school media specialists filled teaching vacancies that would have gone to newly hired teachers. Technicians were placed in the vacancies left by the school media specialists' reassignment. Except for one. The parent organization of the Hacienda Elementary school, Hacienda Involved Parents and Staff, redirected their budget to pay the $52,000 salary of their school media specialist Ms. Dayle Moore. The position of school media specialist was eliminated. As such, her new title was resource teacher. Similarly, the Luigi Aprea Elementary School in the city of Gilroy was able to maintain Ms. Monica Thomas' part-time position thanks to the school's parent club funding her $14,000 per annum salary. This was in addition to $7,000 in previous funding the parents club had provided for Ms. Thomas' employment. A similar story played out in Belmont-Redwood Shores School District (city of Belmont), where the parent organization, School Force, was able to raise enough money to employ a part-time school media specialist for four hours a day at each of the six schools.[6]

---

[6]These are but three instances of parent organizations helping school media specialist maintain their jobs. It is not meant to be a retelling of all such instances within California nor of all such instances of school media specialist threatened with the loss of or losing employment.

> *In the larger sense of dramatically changing the direction of the*
> *state, we didn't accomplish what we'd hoped and expected. –*
> *Mr. Rob Stutzman, a GOP strategist and Mr. Schwarzenegger's*
> *spokesperson during his campaign (Barabak, 2013)*

Recalls were a part of Governor Hiram Johnson's 1911 initiative movement. Thirty-one failed recall campaigns and 92 years later, in 2003, Governor Grey Davis became the first governor in California history and only the second in US history to be recalled.[7] The recall effort was initiated by People's Advocate, the taxpayer group founded by Mr. Paul Gann. Mr. Ted Costa chief executive officer of People's Advocate stated, "We can't wait four years [for the next gubernatorial election], we have to get our financial house in order." Governor Grey Davis' senior political adviser Mr. Garry South defended by stating that this was "the sort of thing" that Governor Davis' critics frequently did (Berry, 2003).

The recall of Governor Davis could be seen as underscoring, strengthening, and perhaps even being the pinnacle of activism that Proposition 13 had set free. The singular idea was that the people could and would have a greater say in government.

Or, given the 135 candidates that were on the recall ballot, it might have been seen as a mockery.

Either way, gone was Governor Grey Davis; in was Governor Arnold Schwarzenegger. Mr. Schwarzenegger, who claimed Governor Hiram Johnson as a political hero, was an admirer of Mr. Howard Jarvis and served as a keynote speaker for the 25th anniversary celebration of Proposition 13. Soon after this speaking engagement, Mr. Schwarzenegger stated he was "a big supporter of Proposition 13" (Werner, 2003) and would not rework it despite advisor Mr. Warren Buffet saying that it should be reworked. Mr. Buffet's comment led to a dip in the polls for Mr. Schwarzenegger that placed him behind Mr. Cruz Bustamante for the lead in the governors race. Democrats and Republicans alike criticized Mr. Buffet for his comments.

The Tax Revolt Countrywide

On November 2, 2004, the state of Maine ballot voters saw a tax proposal identical in nature to that of Proposition 13: the Maine Impose Limits on Real and Personal Property Taxes Initiative, also known as Question One. The principle backer of this tax proposal was the Maine Taxpayer Action Network. They wished to rollback assessed property values to a level found nearly a decade earlier and limit property tax increases to no more than 1% on that newly assessed value. For fiscal year 2006, the Maine Municipal Association estimated a loss in tax revenue between $600 million and $900 million. The expectation was that town budgets would suffer cuts of about 30%. Mr. Steve Norman, the director of the Belfast Free Library and

---

[7]The first recall in US history was in 1921, Mr. Lynn Frazier, the governor of North Dakota.

president of the Maine Library Association lamented that if passed most library funding would be eliminated from the Belfast budget and libraries "of a decent size" throughout the state would face similar financial constraints (Oder, 2004)

Fort Bragg in California was singled out by the *Portland Press Herald* as a real life example of what Maine could expect. That being the well-established dichotomy of those who loved the protection provided against a skyrocketing real estate market and those who lamented the underfunding of services.

Fort Bragg's Ms. Lucile Prince, a resident of the same house for 60 years, paying $700 per annum in property taxes quipped, "It's been very good to me." Ms. Wilma Gromer, an 83-year-old retired teacher held a moderate position: "I like it for myself but not for the schools. I know they need more money" (Bell, 2004).

Fort Bragg turned to fees to make up for budgetary shortfalls. Parents found that they were paying for their children to ride the school bus, paying to support sports teams, and raising money to build stadiums. The school district lost their librarian.

Is this what Maine wanted?

Services thought to be unessential, such as libraries and recreation programs, suffered budgetary cuts. Funding in 2004 was down by 35% when compared with the late 1970s. With more funding cuts to come there was consideration given to a plan that would keep each of the five libraries open one day per week. They expected additional layoffs and had no money for books. This moved the manager of the Fort Bragg library Ms. Robin Watters to state, "I would give anything to have Proposition 13 undone" (Bell, 2004).

Is this what Maine wanted?

With property taxes kept to a minimum, Fort Bragg, like many other cities within California, focused new development on the big box stores, auto dealerships, and strip malls, as they were tax revenue friendly. With less homes being built, there were less homes on the market, thus driving up the cost of existing homes. The developers of new residential properties paid a fee of $15,000 to $30,000 (house size-dependent) to help the city build necessities such as the extension of utility lines and expansion of school facilities. The net effect was an increase in the purchase price of the home.

Is this what Maine wanted?

Fort Bragg was not spared from the tax shift burden. Recently purchased modest homes came with a higher property tax bill than seaside estates that had the same pre-1978 owner.

Is this what Maine wanted?

There was the issue of California's state government taking control of budgetary and policy matters previously belonging to local government.

Is this what Maine wanted?

Proposition 13 was meant to hold government financially accountable. That accountability got lost within the complicated and dysfunctional financial dealings between state and local government because of the proposition.

Is this what Maine wanted?

Could it be, *this* is what Maine wanted? "Maybe deep down I wouldn't mind paying a little more in property taxes but our land and property is the most important thing to us. We don't want to be taxed out of our home and land," Ms. Anne Burham who has lived with her husband in the same Fort Bragg house since the 1970s (Bell, 2004).
Said Fort Bragg Mayor Mr. Jere Melo: "Here we are almost 30 years later, and that proposition has very strong support" (Bell, 2004).
A political action committee was formed to defeat the Maine tax proposal. The committee included the Maine Library Association, American Association of Retired Persons, and other municipal employees. They met success, the tax proposal was defeated with 62.79% voting nay ("Maine Impose Limits on Real and Personal Property Taxes Question 1," Ballotpedia, 2004).
Maine is but one example detailing how the tax revolution spread across the country spurred by Proposition 13. Alaska, Arizona, Arkansas, Colorado, Florida, Idaho, Indiana, Iowa, Louisiana, Maryland, Massachusetts, Michigan, Minnesota, Montana, Nebraska, Nevada, New Jersey, New Mexico, New York, Ohio, Oregon, Pennsylvania, Rhode Island, South Dakota, Tennessee, Texas, Utah, Vermont, Washington, and Washington DC were other notables. Some were visited by Mr. Jarvis to help the tax cutting cause. Similar to California, some had significant budget surpluses or a large tax burden. Most failed to enact laws similar to Proposition 13, although 17 states did pass spending limit laws believed to be spurred by Proposition 13.
I will pause here to note that there is literature arguing the spread of Proposition 13 across the country was minimal. Further, the literature argues against the idea other states had significant surplus.
Back in California the tax revolt's ever-present effect on libraries had not abated. The November 2004 ballot offered Berkeley residents the opportunity to increase a tax adding $1.8 million to the library's budget. That money would have helped the Berkeley Public Library maintain hours of operation, steady the materials' budget, and avoid layoffs. The vote fell short of the two-thirds requirement needed (51%) to initiate the tax increase. In 2005, service hours declined within a range of 28–48 hours per week, the materials budget was cut by 30%, and positions were left unfilled, leaving those employed to handle additional responsibilities. For instance, Berkeley Library director Ms. Jackie Griffin was also the deputy director and a branch manager[8] (Oder, 2005).

---

[8]The inadequate performance of the California Public Employees Retirement System, rising benefit costs, and a marginal rise in existing taxes were also the contributing factors to Berkeley's budgetary issues.

In a more general sense, 2005 was not favorable for libraries as the American Library Association noted: "Many cities and counties throughout California are facing severe library funding cuts" (Denney, 2005). They put the blame at the feet of Proposition 13.

In 2006, the ALA issued a resolution opposing tax and expenditure laws that resembled Proposition 13. It had little effect regarding the sentiment that spurred the tax revolt. Proposition 81, the *Reading and Literacy Improvement and Public Library Construction and Renovation Bond Act of 2006*, being the largest library construction bond act in California state history, and set to send $600 million to libraries statewide, was defeated 52.7–47.3%, needing only a simple majority to become law (Blumenstein & Oder, 2006; "California Proposition 81 Bonds for Libraries," 2006). Its purpose was to build new or expand existing structures and to reignite a funds-depleted library construction and renovation program that entailed 45 projects. State librarian Ms. Susan Hildreth thought it was low turnout that caused the loss, and commented: "If we had more turnout, I think we could have squeaked by" (Flagg, 2006). The campaign manager for Proposition 81 Mr. Phil Giarrizzo offered a different reason. He believed it was a combination of a weak economy, the governor's race, and bond measures on both flood protection and transportation. Mr. Giarrizzo stated, "While libraries rank high, when you're debating costs and need for flood control, highways, and other kinds of vital services, it's a question of how much can people absorb in additional cost" (Flagg, 2006). It was reported that residents felt Proposition 81 was "mindless spending," since they now had the Internet making libraries "far less valuable today than in the past" (Flagg, 2006).

Proposition 81's failure marked the second time in three years that Berkeley had been denied funding. The City of Moreno Valley had hoped to construct a new building as the one library they had was closed due to mold and was too costly to renovate. In San Francisco, were 66% (Flagg, 2006) had voted in favor, they had hoped to construct four new branches. Other public libraries affected were located in Antioch, Escondido City, Fallbrook, Gilroy, Morgan Hill, Walnut Creek, and San Bruno where they had already hired an architect to draw up plans for a new library facility.

Where did California libraries go from here? Some library planners preferred to think smaller and reduced their new construction plans while others worked within their existing structures to renovate and expand. At the extreme was the city of Gilroy. They were to abandon their plans altogether.

No matter the plan, new, old, or revised, finances were needed. Cities were considering bonds, private donations, private–public partnerships, and tapping reserve funds. The California State Library would be working with legislatures to assist in funding efforts.

California government's inefficiency once again spilled over to tardiness as the fiscal year 2007–2008 budget was late by 52 days. It placed as the third longest budgetary impasse in the state's history.

For libraries, late was not better. Governor Schwarzenegger had a goal of a zero deficit. He achieved this goal partly at the expense of libraries as the budget contained $14 million in reductions covering two library programs: the Public Library Foundation and the Transaction-based Reimbursement. These developments came after the Budget Conference Committee had recommended a $1 million increase to the Public Library Foundation. California Library Association Legislative Chair Ms. Melinda Cervantes described it as "a shock to the library community." Governor Schwarzenegger, commenting on the reduction, claimed it was necessary to "build a prudent reserve in light of the various uncertainties in revenues and spending that we face this year." State librarian Ms. Susan Hildreth feared it would impact the amount of funding the state received through the federal Library Services and Technology Act. This act requires the "maintenance of effort" that being the state must maintain support for library programs at a minimum cost of the past three years' average (Eberhart, 2007).

Proposition 13 at 30

The passage of Proposition 13 marks a day when Californians spoke out against the excessive property taxes being forced upon homeowners. The government should never force families from their homes through large and arbitrary tax increases. – The California State Assembly Republican caucus recognizing the 30th year of Proposition 13 ("Assemblyman LaMalfa Recognizes 30th Anniversary of Proposition 13," US Fed News Service, 2008)

Aging is interesting. How things are viewed and feel at the age of 20 take a different tone by the time one is 30. Unless you represent one of the most debated state laws the nation has bared witness to. In that case, age 30 is a lot like 20, which was a lot like 10, which was similar to one. To sum, at 30 years old, Proposition 13 was still a healthy debate.

Proposition 13 turned 30 years old in 2008. Through the years the debate topics and the general feeling of the citizenry has had no significant change. The proposition was still not the elixir to tax ills its supporters predicted nor the catastrophe to public services its detractors insisted it would be. It was given credit for the tax relief needed upon its inception. To that end, a rally in favor of the proposition was set to take place at the state capital. Sponsored by state Assemblyman Mr. Doug LaMalfa the rally's purpose was to inform both the governor and the legislature that raising taxes on residents was not an option.

Upon the occasion of its 30th anniversary, Mr. Joel Fox wrote in *The California Journal of Politics & Policy*: "An acquisition property tax policy makes taxes predictable and removes the problem of subjective assessments by government officials, while protecting homeowners against prohibitive property tax increases. Taxpayers know that their property taxes will be 1% of the market value, in most cases the purchase price, and in the future would go up no more than 2% a year .... After Proposition 13, the certainty in property taxes belongs to the taxpayer."

This certainty also held true for the government. In the first 36 years of Proposition 13, there were only 2 years that total property tax revenue did not increase (Coupal, 2015).

Detractors continued to say that it was unfair to homeowners, local government, and the future of California. Mr. Bill Stall (2008), a *Los Angeles Times* columnist wrote: "But make no mistake, it is Proposition 13 – because of its real impact on state coffers and its iconic role as a tax revolt symbol – whose reform is the crucial first step in assuring California's future."

Many were still troubled by the favoring owners of non-residential commercial property received. They were able to avoid property tax increase through the decades by virtue of a loophole. As noted earlier, property reassessment occurs when there is a change in ownership. For a single-family residence that would be approximately every 13 years. The corporate loophole is not to sell a majority interest to a single owner. Without a majority owner the property will not be reassessed. This loophole, in combination with the fact that commercial property is not sold as often as residential property, has created a shift of the property tax burden to residential property owners. That burden had reached 40% by 2008.

Given the above information, it should surprise no one that the push to change Proposition 13 continued. One suggestion was to apply its provisions only to homeownership. This suggestion had been a recurring theme through the life of the proposition. In 1994 a University of California economist estimated that if business were to be excluded as much as $8 billion per year could be added to the state treasury (Jaffe, 1994).

The mistrust of government had not abated and most politicians continued to treat Proposition 13 as the third rail of politics. Many of its naysayers continued to blame it for everything that would go wrong.

Those who liked the proposition noted that there was more money in the school system since the proposition became law and continued the preference to see it as a social movement that proved the people still have the means to control the government. The citizenry maintained a favorable view of the proposition. Three polls by different polling companies showed that it was favored by a 2:1 or better margin.[9]

Funding concerns did not ease in 2009. Five of the six statewide propositions were defeated. Of the defeats four were budget-related and the other was regarding taxes ("California 2009 Ballot Propositions," 2009). For the first time since the passage of Proposition 13, there would be a decrease in property taxes estimated to be within a range of $5–10 per household. Only five times had the property tax not gone to the 2% cap initiated via Proposition 13. This particular decrease came about due to monetary deflation. These developments interfered with the state's ability to lessen a $21 billion budget deficit (Oder, Blumenstein, Fialkoff, & Hadro, 2009). The deficit was attributed to a lack of political will to cut spending and as usual the revenue raising limitations of Proposition 13.

The failure to ease the budget deficit meant less money was available for libraries. This gave initiative to the writing of a letter from University of California libraries to their vendors asking for a reconsideration of pricing given the

---

[9]Those polls were conducted by Arnold Steinberg and Associates, Field Poll, and the Public Policy Institute of California.

current fiscal climate. Within the letter they explained that some campuses might experience library material budget cuts as deep as 20% in fiscal year 2010–2011. This budget cut would be following reductions in fiscal years 2008–2009 and 2009–2010.

In discussing the fiscal year 2009–2010 state budget, California Library Association president Ms. Barbara Roberts believed that there would be a "huge chilling effect" of the once again late (by months) budget that would weigh on how the funds were used by "cities and special districts" with a resulting effect of "a trickle down to libraries" (Flagg, 2009). However, there was good news as the Public Library Foundation and the Transaction-Based Reimbursement remained stable.

In 2009, Proposition 22 *Ban on State Borrowing from Local Governments* was filed with the California Attorney General. It received the support of many local government groups. This borrowing took funds from public services such as libraries, public safety, and transportation. Providing impetus for this measure was the $11.2 billion the state had taken from local government since 1992 and redirected to California's general fund giving rise to a situation many felt was unsustainable. On a per annum basis it was expected that Proposition 22 would save local governments a minimum of $1 billion.

Interestingly, it put the California Library Association and the California Teachers Association in the rare position as opposition. The California Library Association believed that Proposition 22's passage would keep money from being diverted away from libraries. The California Teachers Association was of the opinion that the measure's passage would divert money from core services such as public education.

On November 2, 2010, Proposition 22 was passed with 60.7% of the votes, thus becoming law on November 30, 2010. A funding victory for libraries ("California Proposition 22 Ban on State Borrowing from Local Governments," 2010; Kelley, Blumenstein, Hadro, & Miller, 2010).

Chapter 5

2011–2016: Where Are We Now?

Same Old Story Same Old Song and Dance

Look, I can picture myself in his shoes after Prop 13 passed. There
was this great fear of libraries closing, of police and fire services
being dramatically reduced. They had to respond. Obviously,
in retrospect, that wasn't the correct response.
– State Senate President Darrell Steinberg, 2011 (Nagourney,
2011)

The governor being questioned for his actions in 1978 was the governor being sworn in on January 3, 2011, Mr. Jerry Brown. Mr. Brown would succeed Governor Arnold Schwarzenegger to begin a third term as California's governor. His welcome reception included a budget deficit of $28.5 billion (Nagourney, 2011) and a debt load that topped $35 billion (Dickinson, 2013), marking the moment in time as one of the worst fiscal crisis in the state's history. Fingers were pointed to Proposition 13 for causing this financial situation as had been the case for every financial crisis the state endured since the proposition's inception in 1978.

In 1978, Mr. Brown was serving his first term and California had an AAA credit rating, the best that there could be. In 2011 it was the worst rated state in the country. To manage the 2011 crises he parted ways with being a self-proclaimed "born-again tax cutter" and initiated Proposition 30. On November 6th, 2012, the proposition won with 55.4% of the vote increasing the sales tax and personal income tax on the wealthiest three percent. Initially raising either $6.8 billion or $9 billion[1] dollars and eventually balancing the budget. (Dickinson, 2013; "California Proposition 30 Sales and Income Tax Increase 2012,"n.d.).

Governor Brown further suggested that control be shifted back toward local governments to manage the programs the state had taken since 1978 and ease the path for local governments to raise taxes.

---

[1]Governor Brown believes that it is $9 billion; the Legislative Analyst's Office estimated $6.8 billion (Dickinson, 2013).

Proposition 13 – America's Second Great Tax Revolt:
A Forty Year Struggle for Library Survival, 95–103
Copyright © 2019 by Emerald Publishing Limited
All rights of reproduction in any form reserved
doi:10.1108/978-1-78769-017-220181005

> *At times it feels as if we are not a full-service public library any longer.*
> *– An anonymously quoted Californian librarian regarding continued budget cuts since 2008 (Kelley, 2012)*

The fiscal year 2011–2012 budget proposal was not favorable toward libraries. On the whole it contained $12.5 billion in state spending cuts within which $30.4 million was traceable to library and literacy program support ("Newport Library Could Lose $300,000," *Library Administrator's Digest*, 2011). This budget essentially cut state funding of public libraries in half targeting the California Library Services Act, the Public Library Fund, and the California Library Literacy and English Acquisition Service. Found within these services and funds lay the money to support interlibrary loan and reference services across library systems.

Regarding the draconian budget cuts Governor Brown stated, "We have no choice" that "we must now return California to fiscal responsibility and get our state on the road to economic recovery and job growth" *Library Administrator's Digest*, 2011).

If the state's revenue projections were not met, by midyear, an amendment would trigger causing all state funding of public libraries to cease to include programs administered by the State Library such as the Civil Liberties Public Education Program and the California Newspaper Project. The elimination of all the above-mentioned programs jeopardized the federal maintenance of effort match.

In February 2011, Ms. Jane Light, director of the San José Public Library said the state money, "allows us to continue this tradition of sharing, and if that all goes away then it's possible the local jurisdictions will say our funding does not allow us to serve nonresidents, and that would be a huge step backward." (Kelley, Berry, & Fialkoff, 2011)

Universities were not faring better. The University of California and California State University were slated to lose $650 million each while community colleges were bracing for a $400 million cut (Kelley, Blumenstein, & Warburton, 2011).

In March 2011, a budget conference committee created a bill to fund the California Library Services Act, the Public Library Fund, and the California Library Literacy and English Acquisition Service at 50% of the prior year's cost for a total of $15.2 million. This would also allow the federal maintenance of effort match to continue (Kelley, Berry, & McQueen, 2011). A move of good intentions that was for naught as by December 2011 Governor Brown announced the elimination of all remaining funding for libraries based on the amendment trigged by the state's inability to reach its revenue projections by midyear (McDede, 2012).

The state's cooperative library system, a networked means for California librarians to share resources, fell victim to lack of funds and was strained to function properly. This brought Ms. Light's prediction to fruition as the Santa Clara County Library District Joint Powers Authority began to charge nonresidents for library cards. The fee was reported to be $80.

The director of the Berkeley Public Library Ms. Donna Corbeil struck a tone of foreboding optimism: "There will be no immediate impact on the Library as this reduction was anticipated. We're still pretty concerned about how this will affect our libraries in the long term" (McDede, 2012). Berkeley did not feel an immediate impact because they had the foresight to set aside money from the Public Library Fund as a de facto rainy day fund.

Oakland's book and supply buying looked to be hindered over the next few months though their adult literacy program will not be. Despite a $65,000 cut they were able to find money to cover the program at least temporarily. Said Oakland Library Director Ms. Carmen Martinez "for now we're just reshuffling some money aroun." (McDede, 2012).

Alameda's adult literacy program was also spared for the year thanks to some grant money. "Next year will definitely be an interesting year," said adult literacy director Dr. Luis Kong in regard to finding the funding to keep the program alive (McDede, 2012).

Still, Alameda, Berkeley, Oakland, and Santa Clara will fare better than libraries in rural areas that typically rely more on funding from the state than their urban county neighbors do. As seen in Plumas County, where basic services such as interlibrary loan, a means to expand a small library's collection, will be lost.

Sacramento cut library funding by $3.5 million from $34.4 million to $30.9 million. Staff were cut as vacant positions will not be filled. This and a volunteer separation plan moved full-time equivalent to decrease from 296 in fiscal year 2011 to 262.5 in fiscal year 2012. A reduction in service hours at the central library and across all branches was the equal to the shuttering of an entire branch. It was expected that near every location would operate five days per week ("Sacramento Public Library Loses $3.5M in Funding," Kelley & Lee, 2011).

The good news for 2011 was reserved for the Los Angeles Public Library (LAPL). Measure L City of Los Angeles Reassignment of Funds for Library System was passed with 63.3% of vote enabling the city to transfer money from the general operating budget to the LAPL ("Los Angeles Reassignment of Funds for Library System Measure L," 2011). This transfer of money was the reason that both police and fire departments opposed the measure. Their fear was that the money would be transferred out of their budgets.

What Measure L did was ensure a steady stream of library funds for the foreseeable future. Expected budget increases could reach $51,677,416 by fiscal year 2014–2015 (Velasquez, 2015). The LAPL called it a game changer (Kelley, 2012). Especially true juxtaposed against Mayor Villaraigosa's reduced LAPL budgets for the three preceding years, 2007–2010. Accompanying the mayor's funding reductions were decrease in hours, materials, programming, and staff. Measure L passed due to city residents contacting city council members to express their anger or disappointment that the libraries were offering fewer hours. The Measure L funding increases were enough to restore the damage done by the restricted budgets. In a twist Mayor Villaraigosa endorsed Measure L (Velasquez, 2015).

Statewide, the amendment trigger of FY2011–2012 that eliminated all funding for public libraries became a budget proposal for FY2012–2013. Governor Brown did not include state funding for public libraries in his fiscal year 2012–2013 budget proposal. Additionally, the governor proposed a budget cut of $1.1 million from the State Library Administration. The rational given was the anticipated decrease in workload due to previous budget cuts (Schwartz, Binette, Warburton, &

Rogers, 2012). In other words, the rationalization for a budget cut was a budget cut. The California Library Association maintained its pledge to lobby for funding (Schwartz et al., 2012). Before the budget was finalized, the state legislature restored $4.7 million in library funding (Kong, 2013).

It seemed that Proposition 13 as the third rail of California's politics may have shifted as the 2013 state legislature introduced six bills that would have changed Proposition 13. A bill introduced by California State Senator Ms. Lois Wolk addressed lowering the two-thirds voter threshold for library parcel taxes and bond measures to 55%. Ms. Wolk stated, "Libraries provide essential services to the state's education system and to our communities. But while demand for library services is growing, many libraries are struggling to meet the needs of their users in light of ongoing state and local budget cuts." The bill did not become law (Schwartz & Rogers, 2013).

Also in 2013, State Assemblyman Mr. Tom Ammiano introduced a bill, AB 188, with the intention of tweaking commercial and residential property taxes within Proposition 13 (Halstead, 2014). It is termed as a split-roll and would create higher commercial property taxes. He brought an interesting look into the many issues highlighting Proposition 13. On the one hand he was a vocal supporter of changing the perceived imbalance in the tax structure between residential property owners and commercial property owners. However, he was not vociferous when it came to the tax shift burden between property owner's pre 1978 and property owners in or post 1978.

With good reason.

Mr. Ammiano gained from the provisions when it came to residential property. In 2011 his Bernal Heights home, purchased in 1974, required a property tax bill payment of $530 per annum. If the house were sold the new owner would be paying approximately $7,500 per annum. Coincidentally his next door neighbor, City College librarian Mr. Anthony Costa owned a near identical home and paid $8,300 per annum. On this matter Mr. Costa stated, "Prop 13 is a tragedy, which has made things in California worse every year since it was passed. The people of California have to settle for inferior schools, libraries, transit, roads, sewers, parks, and other services. I don't object as much to my personal tax bill, as I do the obscene discrepancy between the great wealth of this state and the relative poverty of our government and public institutions"[2] (Stevens, 2011).

Assemblyman Mr. Ammiano seemed to indicate that there was an issue to be addressed regarding residential property taxes, "My feeling is, there's a need for reform, absolutely" (Stevens, 2011). Yet his efforts up to July 2011 focused on reform of the commercial property tax laws and no reform on the residential property tax laws.

---

[2]To help alleviate the poverty, many towns initiated foundations. In the town of Hillsborough, the foundation was integral in the funding of school librarians.

The *Library Journal's* 2013 budget survey (reflecting 2012 budgets) showed that the 31 responding California libraries experienced a decrease in state funding. It was not as dire as it sounds. This same group of libraries made up short-falls in state funding by other sources and as a whole saw an increase of 4.8% in their budgets.

Although it was dire in the city of Pomona. Their 2012 budget was $1.6 million. It was estimated that $3 million was needed to run a fully operational library. They were to operate on approximately $400,000 for the next fiscal year (Plotnick, 1978). In an effort to keep the library functioning the director, Mr. Bruce Guter, suggested laying off near all the employees to include himself. His plan would staff the library with part-timers. Measure X, a tax measure, was on the November 2012 ballot to raise $944,000 (Schwartz et al., 2012). Interestingly, the original ballot title of Measure X was "Adopting a Special Library Parcel Tax," but the City Council renamed the measure's ballot title as "Save Our Pomona Public Library" ("Pomona Library Parcel Tax Measure X," Ballotpedia, 2012b).

The bill was defeated with 60.63% voting in the affirmative (Ballotpedia, 2012b), short the two-thirds majority needed for passage. Mr. Guter did layoff all the employees as well as himself. Still, the library was closed and as of 2014 was reported to be run by volunteers with donations for support. In 2014, Measure PPL was yet another attempt to pass a tax for funding the library. It would add approximately $1.4 million to the budget (Allen, 2014). It failed as well gaining less support than two years earlier with 49.61% voting in the affirmative ("City of Pomona Special Library Tax Measure PPL," Ballotpedia, 2014a).

The San Francisco Public Library received the good news that their fiscal year 2013–2014 budget was increased by 8%. The increase in funding would be used for book collection, investing in technology, a new teen center, and expanded hours. City librarian Mr. Luis Herrera Brown stated, "I'm particularly pleased that the budget is paving the way for the future of our community, with strong investments in a new space for teens, financial support for revising and expanding library hours for the public, investments in digital technology and maintenance of our wonderful neighborhood libraries" (Price, 2013).

In 2014, Santa Clara received a yes vote on a parcel tax renewal, Measure A. This result came at the expense of opposition from the Silicon Valley Taxpayers Association "The whole idea of the library is not as antiquated as the buggy whip, but it's headed in that direction. Are we even going to have libraries like we have them in 20 years? I'm not even sure we're going to have the postal service in 20 years," stated Mr. Mark Hinkle the president of the Silicon Valley Taxpayers Association. Said Santa Clara County Supervisor Mike Wasserman, "The voters have clearly expressed how valuable libraries are to them" (Woolfolk, 2013).

Shortly after Santa Clara the San Jose Public Library received a 25-year stabilizing force by the voters; 81% of the citizens agreed to pass the continuation of a library parcel tax. This was especially good news in light of the fact that budget cuts had resulted in delayed openings of new branches and a cut in hours of operation. San Jose's library director Ms. Jill Bourne said, "Eighty-one percent sends a very strong message about how valued the library is in this community. We're able to grow in ways that people have wanted for a long time now" (Chant, 2014).

2015 was a particularly good year for library related referendums across the country. 148 referendums were spread out on ballots over 24 states with 86% of them passing in the favor of libraries (Chrastka & Kormen, 2016). This is a gain over 2014 when 78% of the ballot measures were passed (Chrastka & Kormen, 2015). Of the measures passed in 2015, 94% were related to operating budgets. All libraries located within the California cities of San Francisco, South Pasadena, and Weed were beneficiaries of the new ballot measures supporting operating budgets (Chrastka & Kormen, 2016).

> *We want a 21st century library on 1970s funding.*
> *– Sonoma County library director Mr. Brett Lear (Warren, 2016)*

The "1970s funding" reference was of course directed at Proposition 13. Trouble began for the Sonoma County Library in 2014 when Measure M, a measure adding one-eighth of a cent to the sales tax, was defeated by less than 3% (2.7%) of the required two-thirds majority ("Sonoma County Library Sale Tax Increase Measure M," Ballotpedia, 2014b). The hope was to restore hours system-wide,[3] upgrade facilities, add book titles, and reach out to "the unserved and underserved areas of the county" (Ballotpedia, 2014b). Measure M would have added $100 million to the library's budget over a 10-year span (Ballotpedia, 2014b), a budget that relies heavily on property taxes. In 2014, property taxes accounted for 97% of the library's budget[4] (Moore, 2014). That number held steady in 2015. Earlier in 2014 library commissioners authorized a one-time transfer from reserves of $535,000. That transfer plus a gift of $700,000 from Ms. Jane Kunde, a former library commissioner and frequent library volunteer, helped to avoid a deficit of approximately $610,000 in the 2014 budget. That was a short-term fix as estimates were the reserves may be depleted no later than 2019 (Moore, 2014).

There was a belief that the failure of Measure M would leave the library system facing a deficit by 2018. Mr. Lear referring to past managerial and financial issues preceding his appointment as director, "To become a fantastic, world-class library system, we need to get away from the year to year struggles" (Moore, 2014). Measure M would have helped.

The chairperson of the Sonoma County Library Commission Mr. Tim May bleakly described the outlook, "Our five-year projection shows a cliff. We're getting by on bare bones through 2018, and at that point, in order just to maintain the status quo, we'll have go into the fund balance" (Moore, 2014).

This ominous tone was played out in library director Mr. Lear's initial statement after the failure of Measure M and then his reversal. First he stated that services "will stay flat." However, within three days he course-corrected and asked the library commission to be open-minded regarding the programs that would have to be scaled back given the financial concerns (Moore, 2014).

---

[3]A want indicated by a petition of 1,150 resident signatures asking the county to extend library hours.
[4]Per Capita, based on public expenditures, the money Sonoma receives was among the lowest in the state.

The library's chief financial officer Mr. Ken Nieman proposed changing the employee health insurance plan and decreasing the funding for both janitorial services and building maintenance. There was no mention of staff cuts.

The Sonoma County Library Foundation, independent from the Sonoma County's library system, was not waiting for increased taxes to help fund the library. In late December of 2015, the foundation hired Ms. Wendy Hilberman as its first executive director. Her task was to raise the foundation's profile and, per Mr. Alex Anderson, president of the board of directors, "bring in even more money to support the libraries" (Moore, 2015). Earlier in 2015, the library foundation contributed $70,000 to the opening of a branch in Roseland (Moore, 2015). It also continued its support of the book discussion group, the Free Bookmobile of Sonoma County, and the library's summer reading program. The Roseland branch, as well as all of the Sonoma County Library system, ran into funding issues in 2016.

By 2016, the Sonoma County Library had received four straight years of increased funding via property taxes as it recovered from the Great Recession. Still, talk of a deficit continued with the estimated date of operating at a deficit having changed slightly from 2018 to within four years no later than 2020. Clearly, the increased funding was not an indication that the library system was in a better place financially.

Mr. Lear had heard the patron's angst stemming from a lack of funding that forced the library into limited days of operation (closed on Sundays, with the exception of the central library in Santa Rosa, and closed on Mondays) and a lack of evening hours. Stated Mr. Lear: "I've (worked) in libraries 30 years, and this is the first library I've ever worked at that's only open five days a week." He further explained the areas that have been left wanting because of the poor funding, "We don't have an education budget to provide classes and events for children. We have book waiting lists that are six months long. We have buildings that haven't been maintained well for 20 to 30 years, so we have about $8 million of deferred maintenance. We're behind on our technology and our IT" (Warren, 2016).

In 2016, property taxes accounted for 96% of the library's budget (Moore, 2016). Since 1978 Proposition 13 locked in the funding the library had received from property taxes to 22.5 cents per $1,000 of assessed property value. Mr. Lear explained that he has worked in other library systems that received funding from property taxes at 35.5 cents to approximately $1.25 per $1,000 of assessed property value (Warren, 2016). He further stated, "We're going to have to establish another funding stream, or we're going to have to make tough decisions about cuts – to the collection and to other things" (Moore, 2016). However, they did not operate without gains to the collection; added in 2016 were eBooks, research databases, and streaming movies.

To remedy the Proposition 13 derived shortcomings the Sonoma County Library Commission sought an increase in the sales tax to be voted on in November 2016 called Measure Y. They were buoyed by a self-commissioned pole in which 78% of the respondents indicated support for a potential sales tax increase for the benefit of the library (Moore, 2016). If passed the sales tax increase could add as much as $10 million to a budget that was stalled at a pre-recession $17 million (Warren, 2016).

Measure Y was passed (Moore, 2017). It was an eighth of a cent sales tax increase that meant the library could reopen on Mondays with Sundays being put under consideration. It also allowed for the hiring of staff and librarians (mostly part-time) as well as the planning of facility upgrades and expansions.

The issues facing the Sonoma County Public Library exemplify that through the decades Proposition 13's effect remained unchanged and ever present. Libraries and other public services have not been relieved of the budgetary constraints that the proposition created. They have merely found ways to manage financial roadblocks.

Since June 6, 1978, Proposition 13 has done the following:

- Mitigated residential property taxes, keeping millions of homeowners, including many seniors, in their homes. This helped to stabilize neighborhoods. Although this stabilization limited the options younger couples had regarding neighborhoods that were available to find a home.
- Diminished commercial property taxes disproportionally compared to residential property taxes.
- Made California business friendly through favorable commercial property taxes.
- Forced local governments into layoffs, reduced public services, and deferred maintenance.
- Forced local government to be more efficient.
- Was a sloppily, vaguely written document that nearly immediately became a scapegoat for many government shortcomings.
- Stood as an example of how the people could wrest control from the government.
- Become the third rail of politics yet politicians attempted frequent changes to it.
- With rare exceptions forced libraries to rethink operations due to underfunding.

All of these points were stage setters for decades of raging debates. Politicians never had the backing, because enough of the citizenry never had the will, to radically change or rid the proposition.

That could be changing.

The tax increases approved at the polls in 2015 and 2016[5] threw open the idea that the tax revolution was on the ebb. The activists groups, interest groups , labor unions, and politicians advocating for higher commercial property taxes had been joined by those quietly talking about undoing Proposition 13 altogether. With the possibility that such a measure could be on the ballot for 2020.

---

[5]In 2015 40 local tax increase measures were considered twenty-nine passed. (Coupal, 2016) In 2016 three statewide taxes were passed as well as hundreds of local taxes. (Fox, 2016)

In 2014, Governor Brown hinted at a major ballot measure for 2018, the last year of his fourth term. This had set in motion the thought that he might be of a mind to join those who wish to change the commercial property tax procedure within Proposition 13. This speculation was fueled by his comments that not having the money to promote Proposition 8, his rival plan to Proposition 13 in 1978, was a failure of his first administration. That speculation was put to a halt by this 2016 quote from Mr. Brown: "I'm not supporting a split roll" (Young, 2015). Still, there were numerous bills winding their way through the state legislature that would change the proposition.

Proposition 13 has caused many shifts within California. Governor Brown shifted from opposing the proposition to proponent. Political power shifted from local governments to Sacramento. Libraries and other public services shifted into austerity mode. Tax burdens shifted from longtime residents to new homebuyers and on the whole from commercial property owners to residential property owners. What has not shifted is the proposition itself. It has withstood challenges, and remains on solid ground.

Is Proposition 13 a perfect law? No, there is no perfect law.
– Mr. Joel Fox (2009)

Bibliography

Adams, H. (1994). *Listeners comment on Proposition 13, lettuce, and fish. All things considered* [Radio series episode]. Washington, DC: National Public Radio.

Adler, J. (2010, March 13). *Debate: California is a failed state*. Retrieved from http://www.newsweek.com/debate-california-failed-state-71157. Accessed on July 14, 2013.

Aggarwal, A. K. (1992, September). Sacramento central library opens amid budget imbroglio. *American Libraries, 23*(8), 8.

Albanese, A. (2003a, January). California universities face massive budget cuts. *Library Journal, 128*(1), 18.

Albanese, A. (2003b, September). CA universities learn of cuts. *Library Journal, 128*(14), 17–18.

Albanese, A., Oder, N., & Rogers, M. (2002, December). Education bond Issue in CA to support academic libraries: Other referenda pass in New Mexico, Multnomah County, targeted rural county; several votes fail, however. *Library Journal, 127*(20), 16–16.

Albanese, A., Oder, N., & Rogers, M. (2003, February 2). Libraries across CA face hits. *Library Journal, 128*(3), 18–18.

Allen, D. (2014). With measure PPL, voters could help Pomona public library turn the page. *Inland Valley Daily Bulletin*, October 29.

American Libraries. (1995a, November). City secedes from Orange Co. library. *American Libraries, 26*(10), 995.

American Libraries. (1995b, December). Another city quits Orange Co. library. *American Libraries, 26*(11), 1098.

American Libraries. (1999, April). San Diego voters trounce library sales tax measure. *American Libraries, 30*(4), 14.

American Libraries. (2000, April). Calif. approves 350 million dollar bond. *American Libraries, 31*(4), 23.

American Libraries (2003c, October). Shortfalls prompt shutdowns in three major cities. *American Libraries, 34*(9), 10.

American Libraries. (2004, April). Oakland, Modesto tax measures pass. *American Libraries, 35*(4), 22.

Avallone, S. (1978, November 15). Proposition 13 reaction: Unions get bullish. *Library Journal, 103*(20), 2286.

Baer, K. S. (2008). The spirit of '78, stayin' alive. *The Washington Post*, July 13.

Ballotpedia. (1973). *California Proposition 172, sale tax increase*. Retrieved from https://ballotpedia.org/California_Proposition_172,_Sales_Tax_Increase_(1993)#cite_note-2

Ballotpedia. (1978). *California Proposition 13, tax limitations initiative*. Retrieved from https://ballotpedia.org/California_Proposition_13,_Tax_Limitations_Initiative_(1978)

Ballotpedia. (1990). *Oregon property tax for schools and state operations Measure_5 1990*. Retrieved from https://ballotpedia.org/Oregon_Property_Tax_for_Schools_and_State_Operations,_Measure_5_(1990)

Ballotpedia. (2000). *California Proposition 14, bonds for libraries*. Retrieved from https://ballotpedia.org/California_Proposition_14,_Bonds_for_Libraries_(2000)

Ballotpedia. (2002). *California Proposition 47, bonds for school construction*. Retrieved from https://ballotpedia.org/California_Proposition_47,_Bonds_for_School_Construction_(2002)

Ballotpedia. (2004). *Maine impose limits on real and personal property taxes, question 1.* Retrieved from https://ballotpedia.org/Maine_Impose_Limits_on_Real_and_Personal_Property_Taxes,_Question_1_(2004)

Ballotpedia. (2006, June). *California Proposition 81 bonds for libraries.* Retrieved from https://ballotpedia.org/California_Proposition_81,_Bonds_for_Libraries_(June_2006)

Ballotpedia. (2009). *California 2009 ballot propositions.* Retrieved from https://ballotpedia.org/California_2009_ballot_propositions

Ballotpedia. (2010). *California Proposition 22 ban on state borrowing from local governments.* Retrieved from https://ballotpedia.org/California_Proposition_22,_Ban_on_State_Borrowing_from_Local_Governments_(2010)

Ballotpedia. (2011, March). *Los Angeles reassignment of funds for library system* measure L. Retrieved from https://ballotpedia.org/Los_Angeles_Reassignment_of_Funds_for_Library_System,_Measure_L_(March_2011)

Ballotpedia. (2012a). *California Proposition 30 sales and income tax increase.* Retrieved from https://ballotpedia.org/California_Proposition_30,_Sales_and_Income_Tax_Increase_(2012)

Ballotpedia. (2012b, November). *Pomona library parcel tax measure X.* Retrieved from https://ballotpedia.org/Pomona_Library_Parcel_Tax,_Measure_X_(November_2012)

Ballotpedia. (2014a, November). *City of Pomona special library tax measure PPL.* Retrieved from https://ballotpedia.org/City_of_Pomona_Special_Library_Tax,_Measure_PPL_(November_2014)

Ballotpedia. (2014b, November). *Sonoma county library sale tax increase measure M.* Retrieved from https://ballotpedia.org/Sonoma_County_Library_Sales_Tax_Increase,_Measure_M_(November_2014)

Ballotpedia. (n.d.). *California Proposition 4, the Gann limit initiative 1979.* Retrieved from https://ballotpedia.org/California_Proposition_4,_the_%22Gann_Limit%22_Initiative_(1979)

Barabak, M. Z. (1998). California and the west; Harman calls for looking at modifying Prop. 13's impact. *Los Angeles Times,* May 22, p. 3.

Barabak, M. Z. (2013, October 6). *Ten years after recall, California still feels effects. Los Angeles Times.* Retrieved from http://www.latimes.com/nation/la-me-california-recall-schwarzenegger-20131006-dto-htmlstory.html. Accessed on October 30, 2016.

Bell, T. (2004). Tax cap? Been there; Mainers take note: California's Proposition 13, while still widely popular with homeowners, has reduced services and weakened local control. *Portland Press Herald,* May 16, p. 1A.

Berry, C. (Ed.). (2003). Groups start efforts to recall Davis; Sacramento A former Republican assemblyman and a taxpayer group founded by Proposition 13 co-author Paul Gann announced plans Wednesday to try to recall Gov. Gray Davis. *Long Beach Press-Telegram,* February 5.

Berry, J. (1978b, October 15). Old questions: New answers. *Library Journal, 103*(18), 2029.

Berry, J. (1979a, January). California crisis. *Library Journal, 104*(1), 5.

Berry, J. (1979b, February 15). Casualty reports. *Library Journal, 104*(4), 464.

Berry, J. (1980, May 15). Proposition 9 a national issue. *Library Journal, 105*(10), 1115.

Berry, J. N. III. (1989, March). Burney's window on the world. *Library Journal, 114*(4), 4.

Berry, J., Fletcher, J., Havens, S., & Nyren, K. (1978, August 1). Tax revolt the library defense. *Library Journal, 130*(14), 1469–1480.

Berry, J. N., Blumenstein, L., Oder, N., & Rogers, M. (1998, February 1). Seattle and LAPL win big in election day bond issues. *Library Journal, 123*(20), 12–13.

Blumenstein, L., & Oder, N. (2006, July). Library bond fails in CA. *Library Journal*, *131*(12), 18.

Blumenstein, L., St. Lifer, E., & Rogers, M. (1998, October 15). CA state library's $86.9 M budget is largest ever. *Library Journal*, *123*(17), 14–14.

Bonventre, P., Kasindorf, M., & Reese, M. (1979). Proposition 13 one year later. *Newsweek*, June 18, p. 28.

Broder, D. S. (1978). Children of the '60s grow upon Proposition 13. *The Washington Post*, July 17, p. A4.

Brodie, I. (1978). Proposition 13 tax cut vote brought gloomy predictions of 300,000 lost jobs its closer to 9,000. *The Globe and Mail*, August 19.

Cannon, L. (1978). Brown rushes to fill budget holes left by Proposition 13; tries to get ahead of movement he opposed. *The Washington Post*, June 9, p. A3.

Carpay, J. (2003). California's Proposition 13: Lessons for Alberta: Market-based assessments are unfair, yet Albertans are powerless without citizen's initiative legislation. *Calgary Herald*, June 20, p. A21.

Chant, I. (2014, July). Public: San Jose says yes to libraries. *Library Journal*, *139*(12), 14–14.

Chrastka, J., & Korman, R. (2015, February). Winning all over the map. *Library Journal*, *140*(2), 34.

Chrastka, J., & Korman, R. (2016, February 1). The constant campaign. *Library Journal*, *141*(2), 32–36.

Citrin, J. (2009). Proposition 13 and the transformation of California government. *California Journal of Politics and Policy*, *1*(1). doi:https://doi.org/10.5070/P25S3N

Cole, D. P. (1998). Special assessment law under California's Proposition 218 and the one person one vote challenge. *McGeorge Law Review*, *29*, 845.

Coupal, J. (2010). Howard would be proud! *The Julian News*, April 28.

Coupal, J. (2015). Blame your officials for busted budgets. *Eureka Times Standard*, March 21.

Coupal, J. (2016). Keep our politicians honest by voting. *Whittier Daily News*. May 13.

Coupal, J. (2016). Grab Your Wallet: It's Open Season on Taxpayers. *Eureka Times Standard*, Feb 17. sec. A: 4.

Coupal, J. (2017). Prop. 13 is the original victim of 'fake news'. *The Daily News of Los Angeles*, March 19, p. 25.

Danziger, James N. (1980, December). California's Proposition 13 and the fiscal limitations movement in the United States. *Political Studies*, *28*(4), 599–612.

De Courcy Hinds, M. (1991). Cash crises force localities in US to slash services. (cover story). *New York Times*, *140*(48620), June 3, p. A1.

Degliantoni, L., & St. Lifer, Evan. (1994, July). CA libraries finally break through. *Library Journal*, *119*(12), 18.

Denney, S. (2005, November). *The effect of California's Proposition 13 on library funding*. Retrieved from http://ala-apa.org/newsletter/2005/11/17/the-effect-of-californias-proposition-13-on-library-funding/ Accessed on July 2, 2013.

Dickinson, T. (2013, September 12). Jerry Brown's tough-love miracle: How he turned around California. *Rolling Stone*, (1191), 39–43.

Eberhart, G. M. (2003, August). Recession, 2003: More cutbacks and closures. *American Libraries*, *34*(7), 20–25.

Eberhart, G. M. (2007, October). California's $14-million library budget cut came as a surprise. *American Libraries*, *38*(9), 27–27.

Facts on File World News Digest. (1978). California voters pass initiative cutting property taxes by 57%; Proposition 13 wins 65% of vote. *Facts on File World News Digest*, June 9.

Flagg, G. (1997, August). L.A. area library systems get good budget news. *American Libraries, 28*(7), 18–20.

Flagg, G. (1995, April). Fiscal crisis may close six Orange County libraries. *American Libraries, 26*(4), 287.

Flagg, G. (1997, February). Supervisors take over S.F. public library; layoffs coming. *American Libraries, 28*(2), 20.

Flagg, G. (2003, March). California Gov. halves statewide library funding. *American Libraries, 34*(3), 16.

Flagg, G. (2006, August). California libraries regroup after voters reject construction measure. *American Libraries, 37*(7), 13–16.

Flagg, G. (2009, August). State budgets hammer public libraries nationwide. *American Libraries, 40*(8/9), 19–21.

Foote, J. (1988, February 22). Going broke in California. *Newsweek, 111*(8), 29.

Fox, J. (2016). Is a battle brewing over Prop. 13?, *Los Angeles Times*, November 17, P. 15.

Fox, J. D. (2009). Proposition 13, thirty years after the revolution: What would Howard Jarvis say? *California Journal of Politics and Policy, 1*(1). doi:10.5070/P2RG6Z

Gaughan, T. M. (1991, June). Good, better, and best are relative terms in Portland. *American Libraries, 22*(6), 483.

Gaughan, T. M. (1992, December). Snapshots of crisis in California libraries. *American Libraries, 23*, 911–912.

Gaughan, T. M. (1988, December). Election landslide (mostly) for libraries in California. *American Libraries, 19*(11), 917.

Gewertz, C. (2004, March 10). Voters in S.F. approve measure boosting city funding of schools. *Education Week, 23*(26), 4.

Glick, A. (2001, December) CA schools, public libraries to cooperate, not cohabit. *School Library Journal, 47*(12), 16.

Goldberg, B. (1993, December). Most libraries fare well in Nov. 2 ballot measures. *American Libraries, 24*(11), 974.

Gonzales, R., & Simon, S. (1998). *Proposition 13* [Radio series episode]. Weekend Saturday. Washington, DC: National Public Radio.

Gorman, M. (1995, April). The domino effect, or why literacy depends on all libraries. *School Library Journal, 41*(4), 27.

Gunnison, R. B. (1984). Proposition 13 author at it again. *United Press International*, March 25.

Hall, R. B. (1990, June 15). The votes are in. *Library Journal, 115*(11), 42.

Hall, R. B. (2010). *Thirty years of California library ballot measures* (1980–2009). Sacramento, CA: California State Library.

Halstead, R. (2014, March 1). Marin shows mixed support so far, for push to fix Prop. 13 loophole. *Marin Independent Journal*.

Harkin, T. (2013). Framers didn't envision a 60 vote supermajority. *Press – Citizen*, December 11.

Harris, S. (1988). Mayor, author launch library funding drive. *Los Angeles Times*, October 1.

Hazlett, T. (1978, July 21). The scare tactics that backfired. *National Review, 30*(29), 887.

Hearne, B. (1885). Children's books; bad children's books drive out good. *New York Times*, February 3.

Hoene, Christopher W. (2002, August 22) Fiscal structure on the flip side: Municipal expenditures and Proposition 13 in California. In *Conference papers: American political science association*, pp. 1–17.

Howard Jarvis Taxpayers Association. (2018, May 6). Retrieved from https://www.hjta.org/

Ishizuka, K. (2004a, March). CA schools may divert library funds. *School Library Journal, 50*(3), 17.

Ishizuka, K. (2004b, April). Voters decide the fate of libraries. *School Library Journal*, *50*(4), 19.

Jaffe, I. (1994). *California's economy, part 2 Proposition 13 and taxes* [Radio series episode]. *All things considered*. Washington, DC: National Public Radio.

Jaffe, I. (1996). *Impact of California's Proposition 218* [Radio series episode]. *All things considered*. Washington, DC: National Public Radio.

Jarvis, H., & Pack, R. (1979). *I'm mad as hell: The exclusive story of the tax revolt and its leader*. Retrieved from http://www.amazon.com/Im-Mad-As-Hell-Exclusive/dp/0812908589

Journal of Academic Librarianship. (1978, July). Editorial. "The time to start was yesterday." *Journal of Academic Librarianship*, *4*(3), 127.

Kartman, J. (1999, February). ALA standards paragraph removed from ballot. *American Libraries*, *30*(2), 12.

Kelley, M. (2012, January). The new normal. *Library Journal*, *137*(1), 37–40.

Kelley, M., Berry, J. N. III, & Fialkoff, F. (2011, February 15). Regional systems at risk in California. *Library Journal*, *136*(3), 14.

Kelley, M., Berry, J. N. III, & McQueen, S. (2011, April 1). California may save state funding for public libraries. *Library Journal*, *136*(6), 12.

Kelley, M., Blumenstein, L., Hadro, J., & Miller, R. (2010, October 15). Colorado, Ohio support libraries in key votes. *Library Journal*, *135*(19), 12.

Kelley, M., Blumenstein, L., & Warburton, B. (2011, August 1). Funding still iffy in California. *Library Journal*, *136*(13), 12–14.

Kelley, M., & Lee, M. (2011, November). Sacramento public library loses $3.5 M in funding. *Library Journal*, *18*, 15.

King, Peter H. (1987). "I am fighting for the other people" Paul Gann: AIDS victim on a crusade. *Los Angeles Times* (pre-1997 full text), August 17, p. 1.

Knapp, F. (1998, October). Nebraska's tax lid discussion isn't exactly a tea party. *Lincoln Journal Star*, *18*, 2.

Kniffel, L. (1993, July). New California budget leaves library service in shambles. *American Libraries*, *24*(7), 599.

Kong, L. (2013, March 19). Failing to read well: The role of public libraries in adult literacy, immigrant community building, and free access to learning. *Public Libraries* (Online), *9*, 40–44.

Kool, M. (1978, July/August). A small town citizen describes: What friends are for. *American Libraries*, 405.

Kristl, C. (1996, November). Palm Springs agreement ensures 5-year budget. *American Libraries*, *27*(10), 15.

Kristl, C. (1997, January). Proposition 218 may hit California libraries hard. *American Libraries*, *27*(1), 16.

Laffer, A. (2018). In Wikipedia. Retrieved April 20, 2013, from URL https://en.wikipedia.org/wiki/Arthur_Laffer

Lawrence, S. (1979). Proposition 13 a year later. *The Associated Press*, June 5.

League of California Cities. (2017, May). *Proposition 26 and 218* (pdf). Sacramento, CA: League of California Cities.

Library Administrator's Digest. (2011, February). Newport library could lose $300,000. *Library Administrator's Digest*, *46*(2), 11.

Library Journal. (1975a, June 15). $$ battleground: Two victories, new skirmishes. *Library Journal*, *100*(12), 1173–1174.

Library Journal. (1978a, April 15). California warns of impact of tax limitation vote. *Library Journal*, *103*(8), 808.

Library Journal. (1978b, July). Jarvis-Gann a healthy jolt? Dissent from the coast. *Library Journal*, *103*(13), 1327.

Library Journal. (1978c, August). Californians ask 85 percent funding for libraries. *Library Journal, 103*(14), 1455.

Library Journal. (1978d, October 15). Grim prospects in California: The failure of SB 2223. *Library Journal, 103*(18), 2038.

Library Journal. (1978e, October 15). Jarvis hits the bay area: Shutdowns & layoffs. *Library Journal, 103*(18), 2040–2041.

Library Journal. (1978g, December 15). More on Proposition 13: Book cuts & frozen salaries. *Library Journal, 103*(22), 2470.

Library Journal. (1979a, January). Basic funding "principles" adopted in California. *Library Journal, 104*(1), 15.

Library Journal. (1979b, February). Calif. survey pegs impact of Proposition 13. *Library Journal, 104*(3), 336.

Library Journal. (1979c, February). Palm Springs ups book $$ despite Proposition 13. *Library Journal, 104*(3), 336.

Library Journal. (1979d, February 15). Sacramento faces threat of devastating $$ cuts. *Library Journal, 104*(4), 452.

Library Journal. (1979e, May). Proposition 13 spurs use of volunteers in Ventura. *Library Journal, 104*(9), 996.

Library Journal. (1979g, September). Balancing the budget in Contra Costa, Calif. *Library Journal, 104*(15), 1609.

Library Journal. (1979h, October 1). Calif. okays long range $$ measures to aid localities. *Library Journal, 104*(17), 2018–2018.

Library Journal. (1979i, October 15). Contra Costa budget inches up 1.5 percent. *Library Journal, 104*(18), 2162.

Library Journal. (1979j, October 15). Kern Co. makes a comeback. *Library Journal, 104*(18), 2162.

Library Journal. (1979k, December 15). San Bernardino $$ up; Chicanos, a service priority. *Library Journal, 104*(22), 2610.

Library Journal. (1980a, February). California pegs Proposition 13 impact. *Library Journal, 105*(3), 339.

Library Journal. (1980b, May 15). Berkeley, Calif. library take $$ fight to polls. *Library Journal, 105*(10), 1128.

Library Journal. (1980d, November). Brown nixes state aid to California libraries. *Library Journal, 105*(19), 2258.

Library Journal. (1981a, April 15). Calif. community programming hurt by Proposition 13. *Library Journal, 106*(8), 840.

Library Journal. (1981b, September). Los Angeles Co. shows how to communicate fiscal gloom. *Library Journal, 106*(15), 1591.

Library Journal. (1982, September). Threat to California library aid. *Library Journal, 107*(15), 1584.

Library Journal. (1983, March). California hedges on SB 358 funding; modest cost of living increase given. *Library Journal, 108*(5), 440.

Library Journal. (1984a, September 15). California state library budget boosted by over $10 million. *Library Journal, 109*(15), 1708.

Library Journal. (1984b, September 15). Oklahoma tax revolt drive menaces public libraries. *Library Journal, 109*(15), 1708.

Library Journal. (1987a, March). Governor's 1987–88 budget released in California. *Library Journal, 112*(4), 18.

Library Journal. (1987b, September 15). Calif. state library gets increases for literacy & more. *Library Journal, 112*(15), 22.

Los Angeles Times. (1978). Prop. 13 is the original victim of 'fake news'. *The Daily News of Los Angeles*, March 19, p. 25.

Los Angeles Times. (1988). Some key players reflect on impact of Proposition 13. *Los Angeles Times* (pre-1997 full text), January 17, p. 6.

Los Angeles Times. (1998). Prop. 13: The need for reform. *Los Angeles Times*, May 26, p. 4.

Marquand, B., & Lifer, Evan St. (1994, February). CA cty. struggles to save PL system. *Library Journal, 119*(2), 21.

Martin, I. (2006, September). Does school finance litigation cause taxpayer revolt? Serrano and Proposition 13. *Law & Society Review, 40*(3), 525–558.

Mathews, J. (1981). After three years of Proposition 13 Californians seek to bolster services. *The Washington Post*, May 29, p. A10.

Mathews, J. (1988). California transformed by 'Prop 13'; voters shape politics through initiatives. *The Washington Post*, May 13, p. A1.

May, P. (2003). Controversial California property tax measure turns 25. *Knight Ridder Tribune Business News*, May 11, p. 1.

McDede, H. (2012, February 5). *Goodbye state funding for California libraries*. Retrieved from http://kalw.org/post/goodbye-state-funding-california-libraries#stream/0. Accessed on July 12, 2013.

McNulty, J. (1988). Proposition 13 still being felt 10 years later. *The Associated Press*, June 5.

McQuiston, J. T. (1989). Paul Gann, co-author of California tax revolt measure, dies at 77. *New York Times*, September 12.

Moore, D. (2014). Library patrons, advocates pin hopes on Measure M. *The Press Democrat*, October 19.

Moore, D. (2015). Sonoma County library foundation hires Wendy Hilberman as first executive director. *The Press Democrat*, December 29.

Moore, D. (2016). Sonoma County library plan envisions expanded services. *The Press Democrat*, February 1.

Moore, D. (2017). Cloverdale library reopens to raves over renovations. *The Press Democrat*, January 8.

Moore, S. (1998). Proposition 13 Then, Now and Forever. Cato Institute, July 30. Web. 06 July 2017.

Morrison, P. (2012). "BLOG: Opinion L.A.: Jerry Brown and the ghost of Proposition 13." *Los Angeles Times*, March 20 .

Nagourney, A. (2011, January 9). Tax cuts from '70s confront brown again in California. *New York Times*, January 9 p. A21.

National Public Radio (NPR). (1993, May 6). *Controversy over California's Proposition 13*. National Public Radio (Morning Edition), p. 1. Washington, DC: NPR.

Neal R. (1998, July 6). Prop 13 terrors: They'd do it again. *Nation's Cities Weekly, 21*(27), 4.

Norris, F. (1994). Orange County's bankruptcy: The overview; Orange County crisis jolts bond market." *New York Times*, December 8.

Oder, N. (2005, March 15). Berkeley budget cuts spur job fears. *Library Journal, 130*(5), 16–17.

Oder, N., Blumenstein, L., Fialkoff, F., & Hadro, J. (2009, June 15). NewsDesk. *Library Journal, 134*(11), 15.

Oder, N., & Rogers, M. (2004, March 15). Budget roundup: Cuts have impact. *Library Journal, 129*(5), 20.

Olson, R., & Randy, M. (1995). Orange County PL pares down after county goes bankrupt. *School Library Journal, 41*(5), 17.

O'Malley, M. (1996, December). *Understanding Proposition 218*. Retrieved from http://www.lao.ca.gov/1996/120196_prop_218/understanding_prop218_1296.html. Accessed on August 13, 2013.

Ousley-Swank, R. (2016). Understanding school library funding: A brief history. *CSLA Journal, 40*(1), 24–28.

Parikh, N. (1980, June 15). Organizing for political change. *Library Journal, 105*(12), 1362.

Patel, M. (2001, Winter). Is nothing certain but death? The uncertainty created by California's Proposition 218. Comments. *University of San Francisco Law Review, 35,* 385–406.

Plotnick, A. (1978, July/August). A run for their money librarians pick up the pieces after Proposition 13: Seek alternative funding in face of tax revolt. *American Libraries, 9*(7), 402–410.

Price, G. (2013, July 19). *California: San Francisco public library receives 8% budget increase*. Retrieved from http://www.infodocket.com/2013/07/19/california-san-francisco-public-library-receives-8-budget-increase/. Accessed on October 29, 2017,

Quinn, J., & Rogers, M. (1991, January). Special LJ roundup: The fiscal fate of the states. *Library Journal, 116*(1), 16–33.

Quinn, J., & Rogers, M. (1992, January). Library budgets survey '91: Hard times continue. *Library Journal, 117*(1), 14.

Reagan, R. (1973). *On spending and the nature of government. National Review*. Retrieved from https://www.nationalreview.com/2004/06/reflections-failure-proposition-1-governor-ronald-reagan/. Accessed on July 7, 2017.

Reagan, R. (1990, June 15). A tale of two bond campaigns: The Los Angeles public library. *Library Journal, 115*(11), 45.

Reeves, R. (1994). On the move: Shadow over the golden state California Proposition 13 unlucky. *Charleston Gazette*, January 9, p. P3B.

Reinhold, R. (1993). Budget in California shuffles taxes to close a gap. *New York Times,* June 23.

Reiss, K. (2014, March 4). *Leadership coaching for educators*. Retrieved from https://books.google.com/books?id=p38xBwAAQBAJ&pg=PT210&lpg=PT210&dq=In%2Bspite%2Bof%2Bwarnings%2C%2Bnothing%2Bmuch%2Bhappens%2Buntil%2Bthe%2Bstatus%2Bquo%2Bbecomes%2Bmore%2Bpainful%2Bthan%2Bchange.%22&source=bl&ots=2pljdzFE9j&sig=3DBtPzfD6EIZMyyiqD5czWvrlUE&hl=en&sa=X&ved=0ahUKEwjCsICun5TbAhUB7VMKHa_bCb8Q6AEITjAJ#v=onepage&q=In%20spite%20of%20warnings%2C%20nothing%20much%20happens%20until%20the%20status%20quo%20becomes%20more%20painful%20than%20change."&f=false. Accessed on May 21, 2013.

Roberts, J. (2012). *Shades of Brown: The once and current governor reckons with his own legacy*. Retrieved from https://alumni.berkeley.edu/california-magazine/fall-2012-politics-issue/shades-brown-once-and-current-governor-reckons-his-own. Accessed on July 19, 2017.

Rogers, M. (1999, March 15). San Diego pushing for better libraries. *Library Journal, 124*(5), 16.

Rogers, M., & Oder, N. (2000, April). CA's $350 million Proposition 14 passes in March election. *Library Journal, 125*(6), 12.

Sack, Joetta L. (2002, May 22). As deficit mounts, Davis tries to spare schools. *Education Week, 21*(37), 20.

Samuelson, R. J. (1979). Son of Proposition 13. *The Washington Post*. October 25.

Scherer, R. (1980). Proposition 13's Howard Jarvis: A little to the right of Attila the Hun? *The Christian Science Monitor*, 24 January.

Schrag, P. (1988b, August 22). California II. Initiative madness. *New Republic, 199*(8), 18–19.

Schrag, P. (1994, November). California's elected anarchy. *Harper's Magazine, 289*(1734), 50.

Schrag, P. (1998, March). California, here we come. *Atlantic, 281*(3), 20–31.

Schrag, P. (2003, June 1). The silver anniversary of Proposition 13. *State Net, 50*(06), 22.

Schwartz, M., & Rogers, M. (2013, February). CA senator proposes funding amendment. *Library Journal, 138*(2), 11.

Scott, G. (2003). Proposition 13's impact discussed; panel looks at taxpayer revolt 25 years later. *Pasadena Star News*, September 27.

Secretary of State California. (2016). *History of California initiatives*. Retrieved from http://www.sos.ca.gov/elections/ballot-measures/resources-and-historical-information/history-california-initiatives/

Simon, S. (1998a). A vote of no confidence Proposition 218, local government, and quality of life in California. *Ecology Law Quarterly, 25*, 519.

Simon, S. (1998b). 20 years later, Prop. 13 still marks California life; Government: It reined in property tax structure. But unplanned consequences good and bad are legion. *Los Angeles Times*, May 26, p. 1.

Stall, B. (2008). Assessing Prop. 13; a taxing dilemma: 30 years later, it's time for a face lift. *Los Angeles Times*, May 29.

Stevens, E. L. (2011). Complaints about Proposition 13? It depends on who's not paying. *New York Times, 160*(55455), July 3, p. 21A.

St. Lifer, E., & DiMattia, Susan S. (1992, December 15). Voters provide libraries with election day triumph & tragedy. *Library Journal, 117*(21), 14.

St. Lifer, E., & Rogers, M. (1995a, January). San Jose creates benefit district. *Library Journal, 120*(1), 12.

St. Lifer, E., & Rogers, M. (1995b, February 1). Orange County public library hanging on despite bankruptcy. *Library Journal, 120*(2), 13.

St. Lifer, E., & Rogers, M. (1996, December). Libraries rebound in elections to garner millions in tax levies. *Library Journal, 121*(20), 14–15.

Telegraph Herald. (2003). Recall election prompts review of California's sacred Prop. 13; there is talk of changing the sacrosanct tax rollback. *Telegraph Herald*, August 29.

The Globe and Mail (1986). Howard Jarvis millionaire led revolt against property tax. *The Globe and Mail*, August 14, p. C7.

The Washington Post. (1979). Son of Proposition 13. *The Washington Post*, October 25.

Throckmorton, J. S. (1997). What is a property related fee? An interpretation of California's Proposition 218. *Hastings Law Journal, 48*, 1059.

Time. (1978a). Between the pigs and the swill a California taxpayer revolt threatens official bankruptcy. *Time, 111*(11), March 13, p. 22.

Time. (1978b). Revolt over taxes aroused California voters confront a beguiling proposition. *Time, 111*(23), June 5, p. 12.

Time. (1978c). Sound and fury over taxes Howard Jarvis and the voters send a message: "We're mad as hell!" *Time, 111*(25), June 19, p. 12.

Time. (1978d). Coping with the tax cut California eases the impact with a $5 billion relief fund. *Time, 112*(1), July 3, p. 16.

Time. (1980). Revolt R.I.P.? This time Jarvis fails. *Time, 115*(24), June 16, p. 17.

Time. (1984). Progeny of Proposition 13. *Time, 124*(19), November 5, p. 30.

UC Hastings Scholarship Repository. (1984). *Taxation California Proposition, 36* (pdf). Retrieved from http://repository.uchastings.edu/ca_ballot_props/926

UC Hastings Scholarship Repository. (1996). *Voter approval for local government taxes. Limitations on fees, assessments, and charges*. Retrieved from https://repository.uchastings.edu/cgi/viewcontent.cgi?referer=https://www.google.com/&httpsredir=1&article=2137&context=ca_ballot_props. Accessed on May 4, 2016.

US Fed News Service, including US State News. (2008). Assemblyman Lamalfa recognizes 30th anniversary of Proposition 13. *US Fed News Service, including US State News*, June 6.

US Inflation Calculator. (2015). *Historical inflation rates: 1914–2018.* Retrieved from http://www.usinflationcalculator.com/inflation/historical-inflation-rates/

Velasquez, Diane L. (2015, July). How the Los Angeles public library responded to budget cuts. *Public Library Quarterly, 34*(3), 230–244.

Walsh, Kenneth T., & Kulman, L. (1996, November 4). On the brink. *U.S. News & World Report, 121*(18), p. 20.

Walters, D. (2016). California governor keeps eye on his legacy. *The Mercury News*, April 7.

Warren, C. (2016). Sonoma county library commission weighing tax to boost funding. *The Press Democrat*, July 11.

Watkins, C. (1997, June). Chapter report: "Shaping the debate' for kids." *American Libraries, 28*(6), p. 11.

Weir, J. (1988). 10 years after Proposition 13 power shifted to state government. *Orange County Register*, May 29, p. J01.

Welch, R. (1996, August). Middle class' neglect leads to libraries' decline. *American Libraries, 27*(7), 28.

Werner, E. (2003). *Recall: Hopefuls knock one another. Long Beach Press-Telegram*, August 21.

White, C. (2011, November). Rising from the ashes: The impact of Proposition 13 on public libraries in California. In *Libraries & the cultural record* (Vol. 46, pp. 345–359). Austin, TX: University of Texas Press.

Wikipedia. (1996). *California Proposition 218.* Retrieved from https://en.wikipedia.org/wiki/California_Proposition_218_(1996). Accessed on August 2, 2017.

Wikipedia. (2006, March). *California unemployment statistics.* Retrieved from https://en.wikipedia.org/wiki/California_unemployment_statistics#Historical_statewide_unemployment_rates. Accessed on August 15, 2013.

Wikipedia. (2018b). *Howard Jarvis.* Retrieved from https://en.wikipedia.org/wiki/Howard_Jarvis. Accessed on May 23, 2018.

Wikipedia. (2018c). *Oregon ballot measure five 1990.* Retrieved from https://en.wikipedia.org/wiki/Oregon_Ballot_Measure_5_(1990)

Wikipedia. (2018d). *Paul Gann.* Retrieved from https://en.wikipedia.org/wiki/Paul_Gann. Accessed on May 12, 2018.

Wildermuth, J. (1998a). New generation of activists carries on after Jarvis and Gann. *San Francisco Chronicle*, May 20, p. A11.

Wildermuth, J. (1998b). Prop. 13 the people's revolution 1978 tax rebellion turned initiatives into a political powerhouse. *San Francisco Chronicle*, May 20, p. A1.

Wildermuth, J. (2008). Prop. 13 property taxes in the voters' hands. *San Francisco Chronicle*, June 6.

Will, G. F. (1988). Proposition 13 has backfired on conservatives. *The Toronto Star*, June 6 p. A15.

Willis, D. (1981). Spending grows despite Proposition 13. *The Associated Press*, January 15.

Woo, L. (1988). 10 years after Proposition 13 between neighbors: Property tax bills vary widely. *Orange County Register*, May 29, p. J01.

Woolfolk, J. (2013). Libraries seek decades of funding amid digital upheaval. *Oakland Tribune*, September 25.

Young, A. (2015, October 7). *Brown: "I'm not supporting a Prop. 13 split roll."* Retrieved from https://www.bizjournals.com/sacramento/news/2015/10/07/brown-i-m-not-supporting-a-prop-13-split-roll.html. Accessed on July 25, 2017.

Index

Printed in the United States
By Bookmasters